THE WONDERFUL DHARMA LOTUS FLOWER SUTRA.

Translated into Chinese by
Tripitaka Master Kumarajiva of Yao Ch'in

Volume 3 : Chapter 2 : Expedient Devices

with the commentary of

Tripitaka Master Hua

Translated into English by
The Buddhist Text Translation Society
San Francisco
1979

6/1981
Rel.

Translated by the Buddhist Text Translation Society

Primary translation: Bhikshuni Heng Yin
Reviewed by: Bhikshuni Heng Ch'ih
Edited by: Upasika Kuo-lin Lethcoe
          Professor Lee Hsing-tsun, Dharma Realm
          Buddhist University
Certified by: The Venerable Master Hua

Printed in the United States of America

First Printing--1979

For information address:

          Sino American Buddhist Association
          Gold Mountain Monastery
          1731 15th Street
          San Francisco, California 94103
          U.S.A
          (415) 621-5202
          (415) 861-9672

ISBN 0-917512-26-X

Acknowledgements: Cover: Shramanerika Heng Chieh
                  Index: Shramanerika Heng Ming
                  Proofreading and other: Bhikshuni Heng-hsien,
                  Bhikshuni Heng Chil, Upasikas Kuo Chu, Kuo Ts'an
                  Chinese calligraphy: Shramanerika Heng Wen
                  English calligraphy: Jerri-jo Idarius
                  Frontspiece: Kuo Ling
                  Photo of the Master: Kuo Ying Brevoort

DHARMA FLOWER SUTRA

Table of Contents

The Venerable Master Hua

TRANSLATOR'S INTRODUCTION

In this volume, we present Chapter Two of *The Wonderful Dharma Lotus Flower Sutra:* "Expedient Devices," with the commentary of the Venerable Master Hsüan Hua. In this chapter, the Buddha emerges from samadhi to praise the profundity of the Buddha's wisdom which is beyond the understanding of both the Sound Hearers and the Conditioned-Enlightened Ones. He also states that the Buddhas can preach the Dharma skillfully, gladdening the hearts of all. He praises the Buddha's use of expedient devices, saying,

> "The Buddha uses the power of expedients,
> Demonstrating the teaching of Three
>   Vehicles,
> So that living beings, attached
>   in many places,
> May be guided to escape."

At that point, everyone in the assembly gives rise to doubts. "Why now, does the Buddha, the World Honored One, repeatedly praise the expedient devices..." None of them understood, and the Buddha does not want to explain further: "If this matter were spoken of, the gods and humans in all the worlds would be frightened and led to doubt."

But Shariputra repeatedly requests an explanation, saying that, among those assembled, there are those who will be able to believe and accept the Buddha's words. He asks three times, and, finally, the Buddha says, "How can I not preach?"

Just as the Buddha says that, five thousand in the four-fold assembly get up and leave. They are not ready to hear the final, perfect teaching of *The Lotus Sutra.* He then reveals that, although he proclaims all dharmas by means of expedients, parables, and phrases, it is *not* something that discursive or discriminatory reasoning can understand. Only the Buddhas can know it.

This means that all the previous teachings of the Buddha--the Storehouse Teaching, the Penetrating Teaching, the Separate Teaching--were spoken to lead living beings to the Buddha Way. They are merely provisional expedients. He says, "In speaking Dharma to living beings, the Thus Come Ones use only the Buddha Vehicle. There are no other vehicles, whether two or three."

Thus *The Dharma Flower Sutra* is said to "open the provisional and reveal the real." Whereas previously the Buddha had "set forth the provisional to reveal the real, and spoken the lesser teachings, he now sets all former provisional devices aside, and proclaims the real Dharma, the Dharma of Buddhahood.

When Shakyamuni Buddha was enlightened he said, "All living beings have the Buddha nature and all can become Buddhas. It is merely because of false thinking and attachment that they do not certify to its attainment." So, in teaching the Dharma, he merely uses expedients to help living beings get free of their attachments.

The Sixth Patriarch, the Great Master Hui Neng, said, "If I said I had a Dharma to teach you, I would be cheating you. I merely use expedients to untie bonds ..." In reality, there is only the One Vehicle, the Buddha Vehicle. And the Buddhas all appear in the world for the sake of the One Great Matter: to open and demonstrate, to lead us to awaken to and enter, the Buddha' knowledge and vision, which is just the knowledge and vision of our own true minds.

That is the essential message of this second chapter of the Sutra. So of course those arrogant disciples who clung to the idea of spiritual "attainment" got up and left.

In coming to the West, the Venerable Master Hua takes the same course as all the Buddhas. He has come to help us be rid of attachments; he has brought the Proper Dharma to the West. In his exposition of this Sutra, he, too, employs various causes and conditions, analogies, expressions, and stories, to clarify the Buddha's teachings, so that we may cultivate the Way. He carefully emphasizes points we need to take to heart: It is necessary to practice and apply the principles we study. Mere intellectual understanding is useless. It is necessary to be unselfish. There are no selfish Buddhas! Above all, if we are ever to realize the vast Dharma-body of all Buddhas, it is absolutely necessary to cut the bonds of sexual desire which tie us to continual rounds of birth and death on the turning wheel.

Of all the Buddha's teachings, *The Wonderful Dharma Lotus Flower Sutra* is said to be "purely perfect and solitarily wonderful." It is said, "To become a Buddha, study *The Lotus.*" How can we neglect our study of it?

Now, this Sutra, which contains all the profound wisdom of the Buddhas and which is here presented with precise and timely commentary, has found its way into your hands. So,

"Let your hearts be filled with joy;
You know you will reach Buddhahood!"

Bhikshuni Heng-yin

Co-chairperson Primary Trans.Comm.
Buddhist Text Translation Society
International Institute for the
Translation of Buddhist Texts

City of Ten Thousand Buddhas
January, 1979

Editor's Preface

Buddhist optimism is seen in *The Dharma Flower Sutra* when it portrays the Buddha as a powerful and compassionate teacher capable of employing numerous expedient devices to help lead beings to enlightenment. The possibility of universal enlightenment is seen to exist in the fact that all beings possess the Buddha nature and hence are intrinsically capable of winning enlightenment. Buddhist pessimism arises, when, with a poignant touch of realism, the Sutra describes 5,000 monks, nuns, and lay people leaving the assembly as the Buddha begins to preach.

Why do they leave? Is this to be seen as a poor reflection on the Buddha's message and/or his teaching abilities? Or does the fault lie with the departees? If so, wherein is their fault? Does the Buddha not possess the power to reach even these karmically hindered slow learners, who, nevertheless, are still potential Buddhas? How can they ever be turned around and started on the path of enlightenment?

The nature of the Buddha's teaching and pedagogical methods as well as the causes and conditions behind some people's acceptance and other's rejection of the Buddha's teachings provide the unifying theme to this third volume of *The Dharma Flower Sutra*. Along with these major themes are others such as the relationship between the One Vehicle teaching and the Three Vehicles, the truth-value of the Buddha's teachings and its relationship to other religions.

As in his other lectures, the Most Venerable Master Hua intersperses remarks apropos the newly formed American Sangha and the development of these pioneer American Buddhists. Although made to a specific audience, his advice and counsel remain beneficial for all of those who find themselves at a similar stage of Buddhological development.

Upasika Kuo-lin Lethcoe)
(Nancy R. Lethcoe, Ph.D.

Sutra: (T.262,5b25)[1]

Chapter Two: Expedient Devices

1-8 At that time the World Honored One arose serenely from Samadhi and told Shariputra, "The wisdom of all the Buddhas is extremely profound and unlimited. The gateway to this wisdom is difficult to understand and difficult to enter. It cannot be known by any of the Sound Hearers or Pratyeka Buddhas.

9 "What is the reason? The Buddhas have, in the past, drawn near to countless hundreds of thousands of tens of thousands of millions of Buddhas, exhaustively practicing the unlimited dharmas of the Way of those Buddhas. They are forging ahead with courage and vigor and their names are known everywhere.

Commentary:

The previous prose and verse sections were an introduction to the Sutra, setting forth the Sutra's causes and conditions. Now that the causes and conditions have been related we will proceed to explain the second chapter which is called CHAPTER TWO: EXPEDIENT DEVICES.

A device is a method, and expedient means effective.

---

[1]*Taishō* Tripitaka references for each passage of text are included as a study-aid. Numbers in text refer to Master Ngou-i's outline for which see page 526.

This type of method is a provisional dharma, not a
real one. It is a provisional device designed for temporary use. Real means that it is forever unchanging,
forever usable. However, if you begin by speaking the
unchanging, real dharma, no one can understand it.
That is why the Buddhas of the ten directions artfully
set forth expedient Dharma-doors and "bestow the provisional for the sake of the real." Later, they "open
the provisional to reveal the real."

"Bestowing the provisional for the sake of the
real,"[1] means that, for the sake of realizing Buddhahood, the Sound Hearer and Pratyeka Buddha Vehicles
are taught. After that, the Bodhisattva Vehicle is
taught. The ultimate destination, however, is the
Buddha Vehicle. The Buddha Vehicle is real. The Sound
Hearer and Pratyeka Buddha Vehicles are provisional,
taught for the sake of realizing Buddhahood. Small
Vehicle Dharma is taught provisionally. Later, living
beings are led to return to the Great Vehicle, the
Buddha-fruit. **This is** what is meant by "bestowing the
provisional for the sake of the actual."

Next, let us consider what is meant by "opening
the provisional to reveal the real."[2] At the very beginning, when the Buddha taught the Three Storehouse
Teaching, to teach and transform the Sound Hearers,
and Pratyeka Buddhas, he said, "This Dharma-door is
the very best. It is incomparable Dharma. Nothing can
compare with it." The Small Vehicle people cultivated
in accord and certified to the first, second, third,
and fourth fruits of Sagehood. They were satisfied with
just a little. They thought that was what the Buddhadharma was all about. They did not go forward or seek
to advance. They stopped at Transformation City. The
analogy of the Transformed City will be discussed when
we come to Chapter Seven. Those of the Two Vehicles
felt that they had expended considerable energy in
their cultivation. They had practiced all kinds of
ascetic practices in order to certify to the attain-

---

[1] 爲實施權 -wei shih shih ch'üan.

[2] 開權顯實 -k'ai ch'üan hsien shih.

ment of the Sagely fruit. They didn't know that there
was still the Buddha Way to be realized. Above, they
did not seek the Buddha Way, and, below. they did not
teach and transform living beings. They were "indepen-
dent Arhats." Having realized the Buddha Way themselves,
they paid no attention to whether or not other living
beings realized it.

For this reason, the Buddha began to "open" up
the provisional Dharma. He said, "The doctrines I
previously explained to you were not the utmost Dharma-
doors. Although you have certified to the Sagely fruit,
it's not the ultimate position. You still have to return from the small and go towards the great. You must
turn away from the Small Vehicle and go towards the
Great Vehicle. You ought to walk the Bodhisattva path
and cultivate the Six Paramitas and the Ten Thousand
Conducts, the dharmas of the Great Vehicle." Thus, the
Buddha destroyed the provisional dharmas by making them
obsolete, and he revealed the genuine doctrine.

AT THAT TIME, when this chapter was spoken, THE
WORLD HONORED ONE, the Buddha, the one honored by gods
and humans, both in and beyond the world, AROSE SERENELY
FROM SAMADHI. Shakyamuni Buddha had entered the Samadhi
of the Station of Limitless Principles. Now, he emerges
from that concentration, and he does so "serenely."
"Serenely" means peacefully and with self-mastery. He
wasn't like those who, when finished meditating, immediately stretch out their painful legs and backs, roll
their necks, and stretch out their shoulders. That's
not being "serene." It shows a lack of good manners,
besides. "Serene" means very calm, feeling one's entire
body to be very comfortable. It means no pain in the
legs or in the back. The Buddha arose from samadhi and
he was just about the same as before he had entered
it. He didn't notice that his legs were uncomfortable.

AND TOLD SHARIPUTRA: He arose and, since no one
asked him, the Buddha spoke without being requested
to speak. Why did he speak to Shariputra? Because,
among the assembly of Sound Hearers, Shariputra was
foremost in wisdom. He was the most intelligent.[1] Within
the space of a single week, Shariputra had completely
penetrated the entire storehouse of Dharma. While still
inside his mother's womb, Sharputra won debates with
his uncle. Shariputra's uncle was a great debator.

---

[1]refer to *The Dharma Flower Sutra*, Vol. II, p.107.

He was an excellent speaker who possessed unobstructed
eloquence. However, when Shariputra's mother was pregnant
with Shariputra, she borrowed Shariputra's wisdom and
used it to defeat her older brother. Because he was so
wise, Shakyamuni Buddha spoke to him. Manjushri Bodhisattva, who spoke previously, is foremost in real wisdom,
the wisdom of the Great Vehicle, whereas Shariputra is
foremost in the wisdom of the provisional teaching, the
wisdom of the Small Vehicle.

Shakyamuni Buddha now tells Shariputra,"THE WISDOM
OF ALL THE BUDDHAS IS EXTREMELY PROFOUND AND UNLIMITED."
It is extremely deep;it's bottomless and so you cannot
know how deep it is. It is unlimited because it cannot
be reckoned. It is at once profound and unlimited. It's
a kind of wisdom which is so high and so deep that it
cannot be fathomed or known by reckoning. It cannot be
known through analogy. That's what the wisdom of all
the Buddhas is like.

"THE GATEWAY TO THIS WISDOM IS DIFFICULT TO UNDER-
STAND AND DIFFICULT TO ENTER." Since the Buddha's wisdom
is extremely profound and has no limit, how can one
enter into it? How can one enter the wisdom of the Buddha?
The wisdom-gate of the Buddhas is hard to understand and
to enter. It's not easy at all to be clear about. It's
difficult to certify to its attainment.

"IT CANNOT BE KNOWN BY ANY OF THE SOUND HEARERS OR
PRATYEKA BUDDHAS." The assembly of Sound Hearers and
Pratyeka Buddhas cannot understand it.

Sound Hearers and Pratyeka Buddhas are the Two
Vehicles. Those who cultivate on their own, when no
Buddha is in the world, and awaken to the Way are called
Pratyeka Buddhas. Those who are born when a Buddha is
in the world and who cultivate the Twelve Causes and Con-
ditions are called Conditioned Enlightened Ones.

Sound Hearers cultivate the Dharma of the Four
Truths and certify to the fruit: the truth of suffering,
the truth of origination, the truth of extinction, and
the truth of the Way.

The Sound Hearers and Pratyeka Buddhas (Conditioned
Enlightened Ones) are the sages of the Small Vehicle.
Although they have certified to the fruits of sagehood,
they cannot know the Buddha's wisdom; they don't understand it.

WHAT IS THE REASON? Why can't they understand it?

THE BUDDHAS HAVE, IN THE PAST, DRAWN NEAR TO COUNT-
LESS HUNDREDS OF THOUSANDS OF TENS OF THOUSANDS OF
MILLIONS OF BUDDHAS. The reason the Buddhas became
Buddhas was because, in the past, they drew near to all
the Buddhas. They presented them with offerings and paid

them homage. EXHASTIVELY PRACTICING THE UNLIMITED DHARMAS OF THE WAY OF THOSE BUDDHAS. They cultivate the Way. They studied the limitless Dharmas of the Way of all those millions of Buddhas. They cultivated according to the Buddhadharma. It is not known how many Dharma-doors they cultivated--a limitless, boundless number of them. So now we study a little bit of Dharma and think that we understand it. That is truly the view of one sitting in a well and looking up at the sky. Or perhaps you have read a few books on Buddhism and claim to understand it. That is simply too shameless! It is to take the Buddhadharma too lightly, as too simple. There are even those who have never studied the Buddhadharma at all and nonetheless lecture on the Sutras. That's just to insult the audience. They are unable to benefit themselves and even less able to benefit others. They lecture coming and going, but they lecture in such a muddled fashion that, the more they talk, the less people understand. Some of them explain donkeys as horses and others explain ghosts as people. They can't explain the word "ghost" correctly and they can't even read the word "person." Still, they go around lecturing. If you ask them a question, they might say, "I never read that book so I cannot comment on that." They may stike up a conversation with you, perhaps using lines from the Ch'an School. They say they understand, but they really don't, and so they end up telling you to go figure it out for yourself.

You may wonder, "If those of the Two Vehicles did not understand the Great Vehicle, then how can common people understand it now?"

Those of the Two Vehicles went up step by step. Although we are common people, if we understand the doctrines of the Great Vehicle, we can immediately certify to the attainment of the fruit of the Great Vehicle. It's like studying. Some people begin in elementary school and work their way up through high school and on to the university. Others may not have been to school, but they associate with those in elementary school and high school and find their studies very simple. They understand them as soon as they hear them, and so they can go directly to the university to study. Although we are common people, our affinities are such that we get to hear the Great Vehicle Buddhadharma in the beginning. Those of the Two Vehicles affinities were such that they didn't get to hear the Great Vehicle until the very end, in the Dharma Flower Assembly. At that time, they turned away from the Small Vehicle and went towards the Great Vehicle Buddhadharma. Now, we

have an excellent chance to study the Great Vehicle
Buddhadharma, and to understand it directly and quickly.
    "THEY ARE FORGING AHEAD WITH COURAGE AND VIGOR AND
THEIR NAMES ARE KNOWN EVERYWHERE." They were courageous.
They continued to go forward, no matter how tired they
were. Vigor means that they did not rest. Because of
their courage and vigor, they were well known. They were
not like Seeker of Fame Bodhisattva who went around
seeking fame everywhere.[1] They cultivated vigorously,
and, because they did not seek fame, fame came of itself.
That is why their names were heard everywhere.

Sutra: (T.262,5b29)

10 "They have accomplished the most profound Dharma, one which has
never been before, and speak of it according to what is appropriate,
but its purport is difficult to understand."

Commentary:

    "THEY HAVE ACCOMPLISHED THE MOST PROFOUND DHARMA,
ONE WHICH HAS NEVER BEEN BEFORE." They have realized
the supreme, profound dharma. Such a Dharma has never before existed. No one had ever obtained it before. "AND
SPEAK OF IT ACCORDING TO WHAT IS APPROPRIATE"--They
speak the Dharma according to the beings' potential.
They bestow the Teaching in accord with the people being
taught. They speak the Dharma according to the individual's needs, like prescribing medicine for a specific
illness.
    "BUT ITS PURPORT IS DIFFIULT TO UNDERSTAND." Al-
though they speak the Dharma in accord with what is
appropriate, still the wisdom of the Buddhas is extremely deep and unlimited. Its purport it not easy to
understand, Shariputra.

Sutra: (T.262,5c1)

11-12 "Shariputra, from the time I realized Buddhahood, I have,
by means of various causes and conditions and various analogies,
extensively proclaimed the verbal teaching. With countless expedient devices, I have guided living beings, leading them to

---

[1] refer to *DFS, Vol. II., pp. 318-323.*

separate from all attachments.

13 "Why is this? The Thus Come One has already perfected his
expedient devices and his knowledge and vision.

14 "Shariputra, the knowledge and vision of the Thus Come One
is vast, great, profound, and far-reaching. He has profoundly
entered, without boundary, the unlimiteds, the unobstructeds, the
powers, the fearlessnesses, the dhyana concentrations, and the
samadhis of liberation, accomplishing all those dharmas never
had before."

Commentary:

In the Dharma which the Buddha spoke, the wise
see wisdom, and the humane see humaneness. The profound
see profundity and the superficial see superficiality.
It is said, "The Dharma is proclaimed with a single
sound and each gains understanding according to his
kind." Although the Buddha spoke Dharma with a single
sound, all living beings understood it. The humans
understood it. The spirits understood it, too. The
ghosts, the Bodhisattvas, the Sound Hearers and the
Conditioned Enlightened ones all understood it. Each
understood the doctrine on his own terms and none understood it completely. That is why the text says, "Its
purport is difficult to understand."

Some of them may have understood one aspect of its
meaning, but not two aspects. Some may have understood
two aspects, but not three. The Buddha spoke a single
doctrine, but it included all of existence.

"SHARIPUTRA!" Shakyamuni Buddha calls out again,
"FROM THE TIME I REALIZED BUDDHAHOOD..." What time was
that? It was one night when he was sitting beneath the
Bodhi Tree. He looked up, saw a bright star, and was
enlightened to the Way. From that time until the
present "I HAVE, BY MEANS OF VARIOUS CAUSES AND CON-
DITIONS..." I have used various kinds of causes and
conditions, not just one kind, but many different kinds.
"AND VARIOUS ANALOGIES..." I have also used a limitless,
countless number of analogies to explain the Buddhadharma. "EXTENSIVELY PROCLAIMED THE VERBAL TEACHING..."
"Extensively" means broadly; "proclaimed" means that
he expounded and elaborated upon the principles. The
"verbal teaching" means that the Buddha went everywhere
lecturing on the Sutras and speaking the Dharma.

"WITH COUNTLESS EXPEDIENT DEVICES..." It is not known how many expedients were used to teach and transform living beings. It is said,

> "With good and clever expedients
> He saves living beings;
> He turns the dust of the world
> Into the Budda's work."

The Buddha uses ingenious methods to save all living beings. Ordinary things are turned into the Buddha's work. While in the dust of the world, one cultivates and transcends the dust.

"I HAVE GUIDED LIVING BEINGS, LEADING THEM TO SEPARATE FROM ALL ATTACHMENTS." I have used many expedient devices to guide living beings. "Guide" means to induce. In Confucianism they say, "In an orderly fashion, one well-induces..." If you want to be a teacher, you must have a method to teach your students. If you have no method, the students will run away from you. They'll be afraid of you. If you have a method, then this student will want to study with you and that student will want to study with you--all of them will like to study under you. If you have no teaching plan, however, they will sign up for your course today, and drop out tomorrow.

Teachers who know how to teach can bring in students from long distances and may have hundreds of students signed up for their classes. Other teachers, who are less skilled, may start out with a hundred and the following day, eighty will be left. The next day sixty will remain, and on the fourth day only forty. By the eighth day they will be totally alone! They may want to teach, but no one wants to learn from them. Why not? Because they don't know *how* to teach! If they did, they would say, "Work hard! I am going to give you a test, so you should pay special attention! If you are not lazy I will pass you whether or not your grades are good. I may give you a B or an A, but no one will get a C. If you don't study well, however, you won't even get a D." Hearing this, the students think, "He'll certainly give me a B or an A," and so they work hard.

The Buddhadharma works the same way. The Buddha is a good teacher. He uses all manner of Dharma-doors, saying, "Study the Four Truths. If you study them you can certify to the Sagely fruit, to the first fruit of Arhatship, or to the second, third, or even the fourth fruit! If you cultivate the dharma of the Twelve Causes and Conditions, you can certify to the position of a Conditioned Enlightened One. After that, he turns them from the small towards the great and tells them, "In the future you can all become Buddhas, but first you've got to practice the Bodhisattva Way. You must first cultivate the Six Perfections and the Ten Thousand Conducts."

When those of the Two Vehicles hear this, they think, "So there was the Bodhisattva Vehicle all the time!" and they set the Small Vehicle aside to practice the Great Vehicle Dharma.

If the Buddha had started out saying, "You should cultivate the Great Vehicle Dharma," and not first taught them the lesser vehicles, they would have thought, "In the Great Vehicle you're supposed to give. How can I give my things away? That's just not fair. I'm simply not going to do it." If someone has just begun to study the Dharma and not yet obtained the slightest advantage, you can't tell them they have to give the moment they walk in the door. For example, if someone comes to listen to a lecture and you start talking to them before they've even crossed the threshold, saying, "Do you want to listen to the Sutra? Give me a hundred dollars!" they are going to think, "Oh? What's this all about? A hundred dollars?" and off they will run. They don't get to hear the Sutra lecture, they don't give a hundred dollars, and you don't get any offerings!

But after they've heard the Sutra lectures for a while, they will come to understand that in order to practice the Bodhisattva Way, it is necessary to give. Then they may give a thousand or even ten thousand dollars--a lot more than the original one hundred. When they understand, they will give; if you tell them to give before they understand the principle, it will be harder for them than cutting off a piece of their own flesh. Even if it is very obvious that they should give, you can't just tell them to give when they don't understand the Buddhadharma.

Since the Buddha understood this Dharma-door, he first told them to study the dharmas of the Two Vehicles. "Just do your own cultivation," he said. "Know suffering, cut off origination, long for extinction and cultivate the Way. Cultivate that and certify to the fruit."

They think about it, "Hmm...I don't have to do anything but cultivate and gain accomplishment on my own," and so they cultivate according to that Dharma-door.

Once they have cultivated and certified to the fruit of Arhatship, then the Buddha "opens the provisional to reveal the real." He does away with the pro-

visional dharma in favor of the Great Vehicle. At that
time, even though they may not want to cultivate it,
they've got a taste of the Dharma and so they set the
lesser dharmas aside and cultivate the Great Vehicle.
When they cultivate the Great Vehicle, they have to
give and hold the precepts. Giving and morality are
the first two of the Six Perfections.

As to maintaining the precepts: Those who wish to
maintain precepts are advised to do so themselves. They
should pay attention to whether or not they, themselves,
are keeping the precepts. They should not go around
pestering other people about them saying things like,
"Since you don't understand, I'll explain to you how to
keep this precept here..."

Precepts are to be kept personally. You should not
go around telling other people to keep them. Keep your
own precepts. Don't fail to keep them yourself and yet
hound other people about keeping them. That's just
like having filthy clothes yourself which you don't
wash and yet helping others wash their clothes. It's
also called neglecting your own fields and weeding
other people's fields." You don't work in your own
fields, but you go help other plant theirs. Your own
go to ruin and you reap no harvest. So, in keeping the
precepts, keep them yourself.

You must also practice the Perfections of Patience,
Vigor, Dhyana samadhi, and Prajna. You must cultivate
all these various Dharma-doors.

So why didn't the Buddha speak the Great Vehicle
Dharma to begin with? It was because he feared that
those of the Two Vehicles wouldn't have it in their
hearts to benefit others but would only care to benefit
themselves. That is why he spoke the lesser dharmas
first. Then later, when they had realized their own
self-benefit, they could start to think about enlighten-
ing others. Thus, the Buddha used all manner of methods
to teach living beings to leave their attachments. Living beings had to learn to part with the things they
could not put down--their attachments.

At this point in the Sutra, everyone should return the light and reverse the illumination. Ask yourself, "Have I now separated from my attachments?"

If you have separated from your attachments, you
should separate from them a bit further. If you haven't
separated from them, hurry up and do so. Don't be
attached.

We should definitely believe in the Dharma which
the Thus Come One has spoken. We should not merely
listen without actually practicing.

"WHY IS THIS?" Why should one separate from all attachments?

"THE THUS COME ONE HAS ALREADY PERFECTED HIS EXPEDIENT DEVICES AND HIS KNOWLEDGE AND VISION." He has penetrated the source of Dharma with his knowledge. He comprehends the emptiness of all dharmas with his vision.

"SHARIPUTRA, THE KNOWLEDGE AND VISION OF THE THUS COME ONE IS VAST, GREAT, PROFOUND, AND FAR-REACH-ING." The Buddha's knowledge and vision is broad. There is nothing more vast, nothing greater. It can't be spoken of in terms of numbers. It is so big there is nothing beyond it, and so small there is nothing in-side it. It is so great that you couldn't find anything greater or more profound. It is extremely deep. Ul-timately how deep is it? No one knows.

"HE HAS PROFOUNDLY ENTERED, WITHOUT BOUNDARY, THE UNLIMITEDS...The Buddha has four unlimited minds: kindness, compassion, joy, and giving.

"THE UNOBSTRUCTEDS, refers to the four types of unobstructed eloquence: unobstructed eloquence in Dharma, unobstructed eloquence in meaning, unobstructed eloquence in phrasing, and unobstructed eloquence in delight in speaking.

"THE POWERS are the ten wisdom powers of the Buddha. FEARLESSNESSES refers to his four types of fearlessness. DHYANA CONCENTRATIONS refers to the Buddha's samadhis. Dhyana is a Sanskrit word which is interpreted as "thought cultivation"[1] or as "stilling thought."[2] Through the practice of Dhyana meditation false thinking disappears.

No matter what one does, one should be concen-trated. You can obtain samadhi in anything you do. Chopping wood, drawing water, serving guests--in all situations one can cultivate concentration.

Dhyana Master Yung Ming Shou, the Sixth Patriarch of the Pure Land School in China, recited the Buddha's name one hundred thousand times a day--"Namo Amitabha Buddha, Namo Amitabha Buddha"--and yet he did not shirk any of his duties. He did all kinds of work, but

---

1

思惟修 -ssu wei hsiu.

2

靜慮 -ching lü.

while he was working he was in the Buddha-recitation
samadhi. Each time he recited "Namo Amitabha Buddha"
a   transformation Buddha came out of his mouth. Who
saw it? The people at the time who had the Buddha-eye
could see it. Ordinary people couldn't. Everyone said
that Dhyana Master Yung Ming Shou was a transformation
body of Amitabha Buddha. He was always in the Buddha-
recitation samadhi.

So you see, no matter what kind of work you are
involved in, all you have to do is have a persevering,
unchanging mind and you can obtain concentration power.

"AND THE SAMADHIS OF LIBERATION..." These states
of samadhi were so high and so deep they could not
be fathomed. The Thus Come One has profoundly entered
them, without boundary. There is no limit to them.

"ACCOMPLISHING ALL THOSE DHARMAS NEVER HAD BEFORE
..." He is able to accomplish those dharmas which have
never been before, the samadhis which have never been
before.

Sutra: (T.262,5c6)

15-17 "Shariputra, the Thus Come One is able to make various
discriminations, cleverly speaking all dharmas. His speech is
gentle and delights the hearts of the multitudes.

18 "Shariputra, essentially speaking, the Buddha has fully
accomplished all of those unlimited, boundless dharmas which
have never been before."

Commentary:

Shakyamuni Buddha calls out once again, "SHARIPUTRA,
THE THUS COME ONE IS ABLE TO MAKE VARIOUS DISCRIMIN-
ATIONS..." The Buddha, the World Honored One, is skilled
at   discriminating the Real Mark of all dharmas.

What is meant by "dharma?"

The dharma is a method. If you speak the method in
an ingenious way, you can lead your listeners to accept
your doctrines. That is "clever speech." If you speak
clumsily, you may talk them out of believing. Basically,
it was something they enjoyed doing, but, by the time
you are done talking about it, they no longer want to do
it. That's clumsy, awkward speech. If they didn't want
to do something, and you talked them into it, that would
be clever speech.

The Sixth Patriarch, the Great Master Hui Neng,

couldn't read, but he was able to speak all dharmas
ingeniously. Once, there were two people who were
arguing. One of them said that the wind was moving,
and the other said the flag was moving. They argued
back and forth for a long time. The Sixth Patriarch
said to them, "The wind isn't moving and the flag
isn't moving. You're minds are moving! If your minds
move, the flag moves and the wind moves, but if your
minds don't move, then nothing moves." That's clever
speech!

If you know how to cultivate the Way, you can do
so in all your activities, and you will always be in
samadhi. How did the Sixth Patriarch become enlightened?
He was a firewood gatherer in the mountains. He took
his bundles into town, sold them, and used the money
to support his old mother. He did this out of a sense
of filiality. He did not sit in meditation and investigate Dhyana. When he went to the monastery of the
Fifth Patriarch, what do you think happened? The Fifth
Patriarch ordered him to pound rice. He pounded rice
all day long. He had no time to meditate or study the
Buddhadharma. He didn't recite a single sentence of a
mantra or sit once in meditation. But he became enlightened.

How did he become enlightened?

In everything he did, he worked singlemindedly. He
did not strike up false thinking. Because he made his
mind one-pointed, he gained genuine samadhi. No matter
what people do, if they can make their minds one-pointed, they can obtain samadhi and become enlightened. You
don't necessarily have to sit in Dhyana meditation.

"HIS SPEECH IS GENTLE..." The Buddha speaks the
Dharma with very gentle words. He doesn't put a lot of
pressure on people, saying things like, "Hey! Do this!
If you don't do it, you're in trouble!" He's not like
me, this unfair teacher who has set down a very unfair
law. I said that if any of you got angry, all parties
involved had to kneel for twenty-four hours straight.
Still, even though the law is unfair, I didn't do it
for selfish reasons. It's a kind of ingenious method to
keep you from getting angry. If you don't understand this
dharma, you might find it unfair. But if you understand
it, you'll know that it is a most wonderful dharma
indeed.

"AND DELIGHTS THE HEARTS OF THE MULTITUDES..." The
words the Buddha speaks are extremely gentle and har-
monious. Everyone who hears them feels extremely happy.
His speech seems to be very much in accord with their own
way of seeing things. Thus, their hearts are delighted;

they are all happy.

"SHARIPUTRA," says the Buddha yet again, "ESSEN-
TIALLY SPEAKING" to come right to the point, "THE BUDDHA
HAS FULLY ACCOMPLISHED ALL OF THOSE UNLIMITED, BOUNDLESS
DHARMAS WHICH HAVE NEVER BEEN BEFORE." There are unlim-
ited dharmas which have never been before and the
Buddha has accomplished every one of them. However,
accomplishing is accomplishing, and that's one thing,
but now he says:

Sutra: (T.262,5c9)

19-20 "Stop."

Commentary:

Today we will stop at the word "STOP." If the
Buddha himself says, "stop," how can I continue? So
I won't speak either. Tomorrow, though we are going to
discuss the most important part of the Sutra, the
Ten Suchnesses.
        Since it's such an important passage, I am not
going to discuss it today. You can wait nervously for
a night, and I'll tell you tomorrow!

Sutra: (T.262,5c9)

                                                            21
        "Shariputra, there is no need to speak further. Why is this?
As to that foremost, rare, and hard-to-understand Dharma accomplished by the Buddha--only the Buddhas and the Buddha can
exhaust the Real Mark of all dharmas, that is to say, with
regard to all dharmas: the suchness of the marks, the suchness
of the nature, the suchness of the substance, the suchness of
the power, the suchness of the function, the suchness of the
causes, the suchness of the conditions, the suchness of the
effects, and suchness of the retributions, and the suchness of
the ultimate equality from beginning to end."

Commentary:

        "Stop," says Shakyamuni Buddha. "Cease."   This
means that the Buddha did not want to speak *The Dharma
Flower Sutra.*
        Why not?

It was to be feared that, if he spoke it, people
wouldn't believe it. What is more, they might slander
it and thereby create limitless bad karma. So the
Buddha thought not to speak it. He said, "I'm not going
to speak it, Shariputra. THERE IS NO NEED TO SPEAK
FURTHER. I don't want to continue speaking the Sutra.
WHY IS THIS? AS TO THAT FOREMOST, RARE, AND HARD-TO-
UNDERSTAND DHARMA ACCOMPLISHED BY THE BUDDHA..." The
foremost, number one dharma which the Buddha cultivated
and accomplished is the non-dual Dharma-door. The non-
dual Dharma-door is "not two." It transcends the rela-
tive. "Rare" means that is has appeared very, very
rarely. Why is it "hard-to-understand?" Because it is
extremely profound. This Dharma is foremost, rare,
and hard to understand.

"ONLY THE BUDDHAS AND THE BUDDHA..." That is, only
the Buddhas of the ten directions and Shakyamuni Buddha
"CAN EXHAUST THE REAL MARK OF ALL DHARMAS..." Only the
Buddhas can be clear about the Real Mark of all dharmas.
The Real Mark is unmarked and yet there is nothing not
marked with it. "THAT IS TO SAY, WITH REGARD TO ALL
DHARMAS..." In general, all dharmas do not go beyond
the Ten Suchnesses. To speak in terms of the Ten
Dharma Realms, there are Ten Suchnesses in the realm
of the Buddha, Ten Suchnesses in the realm of the
Bodhisattvas, Ten Suchnesses in the realm of the
Conditioned Enlightened Ones, Ten Suchnesses in the
realm of the Sound Hearers. There are Ten Suchnesses in
the realm of the gods, Ten Suchnesses in the realm of
humans, Ten Suchnesses in the realm of asuras, Ten
Suchnesses in the realm of hungry ghosts, Ten Suchnesses in the realm of the hells, Ten Suchnesses in the
realm of animals. Ten Suchnesses in each ten realms
makes One Hundred Realms. In each of the Hundred Realms
there are also Ten Suchnesses, making One Thousand
Suchnesses. I'm explaining this to you very generally
because this is the first time you have heard it and so
you probably won't understand it too well. But if you
hear it once, then the second and third time you hear
it you may be able to understand it. Why don't you
understand it? Because it's the first time you've heard
the Sutra and you hear all these, "Suchness, suchness,
such a lot of them!" You don't understand them. However,
the essential meaning of *The Dharma Flower Sutra* is right
here in the Ten Suchnesses. Although you can't fully
understand it, you should pay special attention to it.

Now, I'll explain the Ten Suchnesses. The word
suchness in Chinese is composed of two characters:

如-*ju*, "like," and 是-*shih*, "it is." Suchness means
then, "thus it is." "Thus" is a word which points to the
dharma. It means that we are speaking of these dharmas.

"THE SUCHNESS OF THE MARK." What is a mark? It's
very simple, very easy to understand. It is an appearance. But an appearance may be true or false. What is a
true appearance? That is also very easy to understand.
It is permanent and unchanging. The permanent is the
true appearance. It is, as *The Shurangama Sutra* states,
"the permanently abiding true heart, the bright substance of our pure nature."

Permanent means that is does not change; it is unchanging and yet it accords with conditions; it accords
with conditions and yet does not change. It is not pro-
duced, not destroyed, not defiled, not pure, not in-
creased and not decreased. If I say too much, it's of
no use. I'm just explaining it in terms that are readily
understandable. It is simply the Real Mark of True
Suchness, also called "the permanent."

The Real Mark of True Suchness is not something
everyone can understand and so the text says, "Only the
Buddhas and the Buddha can exhaust the Real Mark of all
dharmas." This refers to the suchness of the mark, the
true mark. What is it? I think you can probably understand it somewhat.

There is also the false mark. That is something
that you are also very familiar with. You all know your
old friend. Who is it?

Ignorance! Do you recognize it? Do you understand
the term? It's nothing new. I've been lecturing the
Sutras for a long time, and I often bring it up. Ignorance is an important character. It is like the leading
character in a play. No doubt you are all familiar with
it.

Ignorance is just a false mark. It is not true, and
so it is subject to production, extinction, increase,
decrease, defilement, purity, and so on. Ignorance is
empty and false. It has no real substance. It is only a
name and corresponds to nothing in reality. It cannot
be grasped or seen. It causes us to undergo birth, old
age, sickness, and death, worry grief and misery. In
the fire of the three realms all living beings are
burned. It's like being burned in a fire or boiled in
water--that difficult to undergo. The Thus Come One,
Shakyamuni Buddha, had genuine wisdom, and he knew about
these problems. He made no mistakes in teaching living
beings. Not being mistaken is just the true and real,
in accord with principle. In accord with principle, it is
the true, real doctrine. It is most reasonable, and so

it is termed the Suchness of the Mark. The Suchness of
the Mark has the two aspects of true and false. Because
the Buddha taught them, we are able to hear this wonderful Dharma.

Now, to explain the SUCHNESS OF THE NATURE. The
nature has the aspects of good and evil. There is good
and evil karma which is the manifestation of the good
or evil of the nature. Karma does not arise by itself,
however. How does it come into existence? It is pro-
duced from the nature. The nature may manifest as good
or evil. In China there is a short work called *The
Three Character Classic.* When children start school, it
is the first thing they must learn to recite. It begins,
"When people are born, their natures are basically
good." When we are born, our nature's are good to
begin with. That original nature is the Buddha nature.
However, "The nature is near, but habits lead it afar."
The nature is basically very near the Buddha nature.
Corrupted by evil habits, it grows far away from the
Buddha nature. This means that within our hearts there
is both good and evil.

How do they manifest?

At any given time, causes and conditions of
different kinds will produce a good or evil nature.
For example, bamboo and wood are both flammable, that
is, they possess the "nature of fire." If you just
let them sit there, however, they will not catch on
fire. You have to add a condition, a drill and a stick,
or maybe a match, to get the fire started.

Wood and bamboo both possess the nature of fire,
but if no one sets them on fire, they won't burn.
Without the necessary causes and conditions, fire won't
come forth. In the same way, the good and evil karma
that we create depends upon our nature to come forth.
The coming forth of our nature may be for the sake of
goodness, in which case it is called "wisdom-light."
When you do good deeds you shine with wisdom-light.
Wisdom-light accomplishes all kinds of wholesome acts.
When the nature comes forth for the sake of evil it is
called "poisonous-fire," and accomplishments by means of
it are what is meant by "going astray."

Our natures are basically empty and still, basically non-existent, like the nature of fire present in
the bamboo or wood. They have to be set on fire; they
won't burn by themselves. Our natures are basically
empty and although good and evil are within them, they
manifest only when conditions allow. It's much like the
nature of fire as discussed in *The Shurangama Sutra* where

it says, "The nature of fire has no self; it depends
upon conditions." The fire nature has no self. Fire
arises only when the causes and conditions come together. That's the doctrine of the Suchness of the
Nature.

"THE SUCHNESS OF THE SUBSTANCE." The substance
refers to our bodies and all material objects. There
are three categories of substance. The first is the
substance of the common person and the Sage. Originally,
they are completely equal; the substance is without
the common or the Sagely. This is to take the principle
as the substance, the principle meaning the inherent
Buddha nature.

Secondly, people may cultivate from the position
of a common person and accomplish their Way karma. This
is the non-outflow substance which those who have
certified to the fruit possess. Thirdly, common people
have the illusory shell of the five skandhas which
unites with the four elements to become the body, a
substance which has outflows.

"THE SUCHNESS OF THE POWER." Power here refers to
karma power. I told you before that I had a left-home
Dharma brother who had studied the doctrines of
lecturing on the Sutras. He was always giving lectures.
What is more, he liked to lecture on the eight con-
sciousnesses. Anyway, according to the Chinese custom,
to celebrate the new year, one writes characters on
red paper and puts them up on the wall for good luck.
The idea is that the letters written with the brush
will keep the ghosts and demons away. That year I
wrote some characters which said, "Wisdom like the sea."

My Dharma brother watched me write the characters.
I wrote them very quickly in cursive style and he liked
them. He started saying, "Wisdom like the sea, wisdom
like the sea, wisdom like the sea..." over and over
again. I said, "It looks to me like your karma power
is like the sea!"

He was outraged. "Hah!" he stormed. "What do you
mean, my karma power is like the sea? Here it is New
Year's and you're insulting me!"

I said, "Now, don't get mad. I guarantee you're
going to like it; you'll be happy."

"You tell me that my karma power is like the sea
and I'm supposed to like it?"

I said, "As to karma power, there is good karma
and there is bad karma. If I said your good karma power
was like the sea, how would that strike you?"

He stared at me. "What can I say?" he said, and
he grasped my hand. He didn't get angry either. So it

only took the addition of one word, saying,"good karma
like the sea,"to make his anger completely disappear.
One knows not where it went, but it was gone at once.
Would you say this was wonderful or not? One word was
all it took. Therefore, one word can be unspeakably
wonderful. But you must know how to use it. If you
know how to use it, it will be wonderful. If you don't
know how to use it, you will run into trouble.

Therefore, "power" here refers to the power of
karma. Karma has a substance. From that substance a
power or force is derived which operates in the Ten
Dharma Realms, creating the Dependent and Orthodox Retribution Worlds. What is the Dependent Retribution World?
It's the mountains, rivers, the earth, houses, vege-
tation, and the myriad appearances. The Orthodox Retribution World is all living beings. Where do the two
worlds come from? They are both created from karma
power. So it says, "the Suchness of the Power."

"THE SUCHNESS OF THE FUNCTION." Function means
to do, to make. To make what? To make karma. Making
karma, one may make good or evil karma. Creating
karma, one must undergo the retribution. If you plant
a good cause, you will reap a good fruit. If you plant
an evil cause you will reap and evil fruit. If you do
good deeds, you receive good retribution. If you do evil
acts, you receive an evil retribution. Therefore, it's
all what you make it:

Good and evil are two different roads.

You can cultivate or you can commit offenses.
"Cultivate" means to cultivate the good. "Commit" means
to do evil. The Suchness of the Function refers to doing
good and receiving blessings or doing evil and receiving
misfortune.

"THE SUCHNESS OF THE CAUSES." A cause refers to the
minds of all living beings. The mind may be likened to
a piece of ground. All good and evil are manifest only
from the mind. They manifest from your mind and so
previously we spoke of the cause as a seed. The seed is
planted in your mind and so it is called the "mind
ground." All the grasses and trees are born from the
earth, and all good and evil comes from the mind. All
the seeds of good and evil planted in your mind are
the causes.

"THE SUCHNESS OF THE CONDITIONS." There are two
factors which go into making up the conditions. The
first is the factor of time and the second is the
factor of the situation. The condition itself is basically devoid of good or evil, but it must be present for
a particular appearance to manifest. This may be com-

pared to something which is withered and dry, and which ignites at the first spark. The spark is the aiding condition. It may also be likened to ice which melts when the sun shines on it. The colder it gets, the harder the ice freezes, but when the sun shines, the ice will melt.

When you plant a seed in the earth, if the conditions are not right, it won't come up. You have to plant it in the ground and then make sure the sun shines on it, and the rain falls on it. These are all conditions. They come together and help the seed, the cause, grow.

"THE SUCHNESS OF THE EFFECT." To start out on a course of action is called the cause. If you do something, at the very beginning it is a cause. When the matter has been successfully completed, that is the effect. The effect is also spoken of in terms of good and evil. Good and evil effects come from good and evil causes respectively. So it is said, "Carrying the cause, one realizes the effect."

"THE SUCHNESS OF THE RETRIBUTION." Retribution is the complex of effects incurred as a result of the karma you have created. According to the type of karma you create, you undergo just that kind of retribution.

You may ask, "What is the difference, then, between the effect and the retribution?"

The effect takes place before the retribution is undergone. It's the immediate consequence. One undergoes retribution when the effects have been broken through and one receives recompense. If you planted an evil cause, you reap the effect. Later, you receive the retribution.

What is meant by the effect? If we create all kinds of evil karma and fall into hell, that is the attainment of the effect of hell. Once you are in the pot, you're undergoing retribution. Receiving the torments of hell is retribution. If you enlighten to the principle of retribution, you can certify to the positions of the Four Sagely Realms, the Buddhas, the Bodhisattvas, the Sound Hearers and the Conditioned Enlightened Ones. If you have awakened, you can hope to attain the Four Sagely Positions. If you are confused, deluded, you will bring the retribution of the Common Realms Down Upon Yourself, and end up among the gods, humans, asuras, hell-beings, hungry ghosts, or animals.

"THE SUCHNESS OF THE ULTIMATE EQUALITY FROM BEGINING TO END." In the above-mentioned Suchnesses there are the two paths of confusion and enlightenment. Whether you are confused or enlightened, from the beginning to the very end, the first through the ninth, when discussed in terms of cause and effect, they are non-dual and ultimately equal.

The Ten Suchnesses are present in the Buddha Realm, but they are very fine and special states. In the hells there are also Ten Suchnesses, but they are nothing at all like the Buddha Realm states; they are very bad; they are not superior and fine. In fact, they are terrible!

The Ten Suchnessness existing in each of the Ten Dharma Realms makes One Hundred Realms. The Ten Suchnesses then existing in each of the Hundred Realms makes One Thousand Suchnesses. This is known as the Hundred Realms and the Thousand Suchnesses.

The Hundred Realms and the Thousand Suchnesses include all of the various situations in the Ten Dharma Realms. *The Dharma Flower Sutra* lists the Ten Suchnesses and, also I have explained them, I believe you probably don't understand them fully. If you truly wish to understand them, you will have to work harder in your investigation of the Buddhadharma. After you have investigated it for a long time, you will naturally be able to understand this doctrine.

Sutra: (T.262,5c14)

22-24 At that time, the World Honored One, wishing to restate this meaning, spoke verses saying,

> Illimitable are the heroes of the world.
>
> All the gods and people in the world,
>
> And all the classes of living beings
>
> Cannot know the Buddhas.
>
> The Buddhas' powers, fearlessnesses,
>
> Liberations and samadhis,
>
> And other dharmas of the Buddhas
>
> Can be fathomed by no one.
>
> 25 Formerly, following countless Buddhas,
>
> I perfectly walked all the paths
>
> Of the wonderful Dharma, subtle and deep,
>
> Hard to see and hard to understand;
>
> Through limitless millions of aeons,

I walked down all these paths.

In the Bodhimanda, I realized the fruit,

And have fully known and seen it all.

Commentary:

ILLIMITABLE ARE THE HEROES OF THE WORLD/ The
Buddhas possess great heroism, great strength, great
kindness, and great compassion. No one can measure
the states of the Buddhas.

ALL THE GODS AND PEOPLE IN THE WORLD/ AND ALL THE
CLASSES OF LIVING BEINGS/ CANNOT KNOW THE BUDDHAS/
There is not a single living being that can know the
realm of the Buddhas, that can know the spiritual powers
and wonderful functions of the Buddhas.

THE BUDDHAS' POWERS, FEARLESSNESSES/ LIBERATIONS
AND SAMADHIS/ AND OTHER DHARMAS OF THE BUDDHAS/ CAN BE
FATHOMED BY NO ONE/ The Buddhas have Ten Wisdom Powers,
Four Fearlessnesses, Eight Liberations and countless
samadhis. There isn't anyone who can fathom all the
wonderful Dharmas of the Buddhas.

FORMERLY, FOLLOWING COUNTLESS BUDDHAS/ "Formerly"
means in the causal ground, limitless aeons ago. I
PERFECTLY WALKED ALL THE PATHS/ I cultivated all the
Dharma-doors OF THE WONDERFUL DHARMA, SUBTLE AND DEEP/
The Dharma is extremely subtle and profound. How deep is
it? No one knows. HARD TO SEE AND HARD TO UNDERSTAND/
This Dharma is difficult to encounter in a hundred
thousand aeons. It is difficult to understand. And so
the Four Vast Vows run:

> Living beings are boundless,
>   I vow to save them.
> Afflictions are endless,
>   I vow to sever them.
> Dharma-doors are limitless,
>   I vow to master them.
> The Buddha Way is supreme,
>   I vow to realize it.

In the causal ground, the Buddha made these Four Vast
Vows in every life and cultivated the Way. The Dharma
which he realized is not easy to understand.

THROUGH LIMITLESS MILLIONS OF AEONS/ I WALKED DOWN
ALL THESE PATHS/ I cultivated the Thirty-seven Limbs of
Enlightenment. They are: the Five Roots, the Five Powers,
the Four Applications of Mindfulness, the Four Right
Efforts, the Four As-you-will Fulfillments, the Seven
Bodhi Shares, and the Eightfold Path. That's thirty-
seven. You can also include the Four Truths, the Twelve

Causes and Conditions, the Six Perfections and the Ten
Thousand Conducts.

   IN THE BODHIMANDA I REALIZED THE FRUIT/ Because I
cultivated all these Dharmas, in the Bodhimanda I
realized Buddhahood. AND HAVE FULLY KNOWN AND SEEN IT
ALL/ I have seen all there is to see and I know all
there is to know.

Sutra: (T.262,5c23)

26-27 The great effect and retribution,

   The various natures, marks, and meanings,

   Are such that I and the ten-direction Buddhas

   Alone can understand these matters.

Commentary:

   THE GREAT EFFECT AND RETRIBUTION/ Supreme, right
enlightenment is the great effect. The perfect, full
reward body is the great retribution. THE VARIOUS
NATURES, MARKS AND MEANINGS/ This refers to the doctrine
of the Ten Suchnesses. ARE SUCH THAT I AND THE TEN-
DIRECTION BUDDHAS/ ALONE CAN UNDERSTAND THESE MATTERS/
Only the Buddhas can understand these matters.

Sutra: (T.262,5c25)

28 This Dharma can't be demonstrated,

   The mark of language being still and extinct;

   Of all the kinds of living beings

   None there is who can understand it.

   Except the host of Bodhisattvas,

   Firm in the power of faith.

   The host of the Buddha's disciples

   Who've made offerings to the Buddhas

   And who have exhausted all outflows,

   And dwell in their final bodies--

   The strength of people such as these

   Also proves inadequate.

   If the world were filled

   With those like Shariputra,

Who together spent their thoughts to measure it,
They couldn't fathom the Buddha's wisdom.

Commentary:

THIS DHARMA CAN'T BE DEMONSTRATED/ You can't just
casually speak this wonderful Dharma to people. Why not?
Because of THE MARK OF LANGUAGE BEING STILL AND EXTINCT/
this is the ultimate Real Mark Dharma-door where the
path of words and language is cut off. It has already
been severed. The place where the mind functions has
been dispensed with.

> The mouth wants to speak
>   but words fail;
> The mind wants to think,
>   but thoughts are lost.

The mind wants to climb on conditions and scheme, but
the thoughts just aren't there. The thoughts have died
as well.

> The path of words and language is cut off;
> The place of the mind's functioning is gone.

There's nothing to say. The true, wonderful Dharma is
ineffable. It cannot be expressed in words because it
is something within the self-nature. It is not found
outside. In this wonderful Dharma, "the marks of
language are still and extinct."

OF ALL THE KINDS OF LIVING BEINGS/ NONE THERE IS
WHO CAN UNDERSTAND IT/ EXCEPT THE HOST OF BODHISATTVAS/
FIRM IN THE POWER OF FAITH/ Not one single kind of
living being can understand this wonderful Dharma,
except for the Great Vehicle Bodhisattvas. Because the
Bodhisattvas have hearts full of faith, they can understand the Real Mark Dharma. People like Bodhisattva
Manjushri can understand this Dharma. They may not understand it totally, but they believe in it.

THE HOST OF THE BUDDHA'S DISCIPLES/ WHO'VE MADE
OFFERINGS TO THE BUDDHAS/ who have, in former lives,
made offerings to all the Buddhas AND WHO HAVE EXHAUSTED
ALL OUTFLOWS/ They have obtained to non-outflows,
certified to the attainment of Pratyeka Buddhahood
AND DWELL IN THEIR FINAL BODIES/ They now inhabit their
very last retribution bodies. After this, they will
undergo no further becoming. THE STRENGTH OF PERSONS
SUCH AS THESE/ People like the Bodhisattvas and the
Pratyeka Buddhas ALSO PROVES INADEQUATE/ They can't
understand this Buddhadharma either.

IF THE WORLD WERE FILLED/ WITH THOSE LIKE SHARIPUTRA
Let's suppose the whole world was filled with people

who had as much wisdom as Shariputra, the wisest of the
Buddha's disciples, WHO TOGETHER SPENT THEIR THOUGHTS TO
MEASURE IT/ If they exhausted their thoughts and the
power of their wisdom trying to plumb the depths of the
Buddha's wisdom, they couldn't do it. They could never
fathom the Buddha's inconceivable, subtle, and wonderful
Dharma. THEY COULDN'T FATHOM THE BUDDHA'S WISDOM/ They
would be unable to comprehend the wisdom of the Buddha.

Sutra: (T.262,6a4)

> Truly, suppose the ten directions,
> Were filled with those like Shariputra,
> And that the remaining disciples filled
> All the lands in the ten directions,
> And that together they spent their thoughts to measure it,
> They also could not know it.
> If Pratyeka Buddhas of sharp wisdom
> Without outflows, in their final bodies,
> Also filled the ten-directions,
> Their number like the bamboo in the forest,
> And if they put their minds together,
> Wishing to think about the Buddha's real wisdom,
> Throughout measureless millions aeons,
> They could not know the smallest part of it.
> Suppose newly resolved Bodhisattvas,
> Who've made offerings to countless Buddhas,
> Who understand the principle and the purport,
> And are well able to speak the Dharma,
> Whose numbers are like rice, hemp, bamboo, and reeds,
> Filled the ten-direction lands,
> And suppose with one mind and with wondrous wisdom,
> They were all together to think it over,
> Throughout aeons like the Ganges' sands,
> Even they couldn't know the Buddha's wisdom.

Commentary:

The Buddha has two types of wisdom, the provisional
and the real.   Provisional wisdom is used to speak the
Dharma in accord with conditions and to use expedient
devices to take living beings across. Real wisdom is
genuine, Real Mark wisdom.

TRULY, SUPPOSE THE TEN DIRECTIONS/ Previously
it just said "the world," meaning one world. Here it
says "the ten directions" meaning all the worlds in
the ten directions. WERE FILLED WITH THOSE LIKE SHARI-
PUTRA/ If living beings of the ten-direction worlds were
all as intelligent as Shariputra...Shariputra's wisdom,
however, is provisional wisdom; it is not real wisdom.

AND THAT THE REMAINING DISCIPLES FILLED/ ALL THE
LANDS IN THE TEN DIRECTIONS/ AND THAT TOGETHER THEY SPEN'
THEIR THOUGHTS TO MEASURE IT/ THEY ALSO COULD NOT KNOW
IT/ If Shariputra and all the other disciples spent
their thoughts, exhausted their brains, to calculate
the Buddha's wisdom, they couldn't know it. They could
never fathom the Buddha's real wisdom.

IF PRATYEKA BUDDHAS OF SHARP WISDOM/Previously,
the Sound Hearers were spoken of. Here, we speak of
the Pratyeka Buddhas who are a bit higher in wisdom.
WITHOUT OUTFLOWS, IN THEIR FINAL BODIES/ ALSO FILLED
THE TEN DIRECTIONS/ They have already attained to the
state of no-outflows, the Penetration of the Extinction
of Outflows, and they dwell in their last retribution
bodies. Once one has certified to the fruit of Pratyeka
Buddhahood, one does not again receive a retribution
body. So, this is their very last retribution body.
THEIR NUMBER LIKE THE BAMBOO IN THE FOREST/ If they
numbered as many as the bamboo in the bamboo groves,
AND **IF THEY PUT THEIR MINDS TOGETHER**/ WISHING TO THINK
ABOUT THE BUDDHA'S REAL WISDOM/ THEY COULD NOT KNOW THE
SMALLEST PART OF IT/ To say nothing of understanding
it completely, they couldn't even know the tiniest, most
minute portion thereof.

SUPPOSE NEWLY REVOLED BODHISATTVAS/ Bodhisattvas
who have just brought forth their hearts, WHO'VE MADE
OFFERINGS TO COUNTLESS BUDDHAS/ WHO UNDERSTAND THE
PRINCIPLE AND THE PURPORT/ AND ARE WELL ABLE TO SPEAK
THE DHARMA/ They have unimpeded comprehension of the
Buddhadharma's doctrines. Not only that, but they are
well-qualified speakers of the Dharma and possess un-
obstructed eloquence. WHOSE NUMBERS ARE LIKE RICE,HEMP,
BAMBOO, AND REEDS/ FILLED THE TEN DIRECTIONS LANDS/ AND
SUPPOSE WITH ONE MIND AND WITH WONDROUS WISDOM/If they
combined their hearts into one and used that fine and

subtle wisdom. THROUGHOUT AEONS LIKE THE GANGES' SANDS/
EVEN THEY COULDN'T KNOW THE BUDDHA'S WISDOM/ If they all
got together to try to calculate the Buddha's wisdom,
they couldn't do it.

Sutra: (*T.262,6a16*)

    Suppose that non-retreating Bodhisattvas,

    Their number like the Ganges' sands,

    With one mind thought to seek that wisdom

    They also could not know of it.

29
    And what is more, Shariputra,

    That inconceivable, non-outflow,

    Most profound and subtle Dharma,

    I have perfectly obtained,

    And I alone know its mark,

    Along with the ten-direction Buddhas.

30-31 Shariputra, you should know

    The words of the Buddhas do not differ.

    In the Dharma spoken by the Buddhas

    You should place the power of great faith.

    When the World Honored One's Dharma's at its end,

    The true and real must be spoken.

32
    I tell the assembly of Sound Hearers

    And those who seek the Conditioned Enlightened Vehicle,

    That I will lead them to cast off suffering's bond,

    And arrive at Nirvana.

    The Buddha uses the power of expedients,

    Demonstrating the teaching of Three Vehicles,

    So that living beings, attached in many places,

    May be guided to escape.

Commentary:

    SUPPOSE THAT NON-RETREATING BODHISATTVAS/ Above,
the newly-resolved Bodhisattvas, the Sound Hearers, and
the Conditioned Enlightened Ones were mentioned. Some-

times newly-resolved Bodhisattvas may retreat and lose
their Bodhi-hearts. Sound Hearers may become "fixed-
Sound Hearers," that is, fixed at the position of
Sound Hearer. Other Sound Hearers are those who have
retreated from the Great Vehicle; they brought forth
the Bodhisattva heart, but then they retreated to the
Sound Hearer position. Some have brought forth the
Bodhisattva heart, but do not as yet have any genuine
samadhi power. Those are the newly-resolved Bodhisattvas.

This passage of text mentions non-retreating Bodhisattvas. They will never retreat to the Two Vehicles.
They cultivate the Great Vehicle Dharma-doors and will
never again go back to the lesser vehicles. THEIR
NUMBER LIKE THE GANGES' SANDS/ There were a great many
non-retreating Bodhisattvs, let's say...There are
three levels of non-retreat:

1. Non-retreating position: This means that the
Great Vehicle Bodhisattva will never go back to the
position of either of the Two Vehicles.

2. Non-retreating conduct: This means that, in
their cultivation, the Great Vehicle Bodhisattvas are
always vigorous and never lazy; they advance with
heroic vigor.

3. Non-retreating thought: Not only do they not
retreat in their position or their cultivation, but they
don't even have the thought of doing so.

WITH ONE MIND THOUGHT TO SEEK THAT WISDOM/ If they
got together and investigated the Buddha's wisdom, the
real wisdom THEY ALSO COULD NOT KNOW OF IT/ Although
they occupy a position from which they do not retreat,
they still haven't obtained the true, real wisdom. Their
wisdom is merely provisional. They cannot understand
the Buddha's true, real wisdom.

AND WHAT IS MORE, SHARIPUTRA/ The Buddha further
addresses Shariputra, THAT INCONCEIVABLE, NON-OUTFLOW/
MOST PROFOUND AND SUBTLE DHARMA/ The real mark of all
Dharmas, the true, real wisdom, the spiritual penetration
of non-outflows is inconceivable. It can't be thought of
with the mind or expressed in words. It is extremely deep
subtle, and wonderful. This Dharma is unsurpassed and
also extremely deep, at once fine and subtle. It's extremely wonderful and inconceivable. I HAVE PERFECTLY
OBTAINED/ It is perfect, neither lacking nor in excess.
AND I ALONE KNOW ITS MARK/ Only Shakyamuni Buddha can
know the real wisdom. ALONG WITH THE TEN-DIRECTION
BUDDHAS/ All those in the ten directions who have realized Buddhahood can know it. So it said above, "Only
the Buddhas and the Buddha can exhaust the Real Mark of
all dharmas..." The meaning is the same here.

SHARIPUTRA, YOU SHOULD KNOW/ THE WORDS OF THE
BUDDHAS DO NOT DIFFER/ What all the Buddhas say is true,
real speech; it is the same sound spoken with different
mouths. The Thus Come One speaks the truth, speaks of
what is, he speaks it truly and he never speaks
falsely. The path of all the Buddhas is identical.
Therefore, the Dharma which the Buddhas speak is the
same. The Buddha's true, real wisdom can be known and
understood only by the Buddhas and the Buddha.

IN THE DHARMA SPOKEN BY THE BUDDHAS/ YOU SHOULD
PLACE THE POWER OF GREAT FAITH/ You should have no
doubts, only faith. Faith is extremely powerful. Why
do you need faith? It is said,

> The Buddhadharma is like the great sea;
> You can only enter it by means of faith.

If you don't have faith, you won't be able to understand the doctrines within the Buddhadharma.

> Faith is the source of the Way,
> And the mother of merit and virtue.
> It nourishes all our good roots.

Faith will nourish your good roots. Without it, they
cannot grow. Faith is extremely important. If you listen
to the Sutras, you must believe what they say. If you
don't believe them, it is just as if you hadn't heard
them. We should believe in the Dharma the Buddha spoke.
If we don't, it is just as if we never even heard it.

WHEN THE WORLD HONORED ONE'S DHARMA'S AT ITS END/
After the World Honored One realized Buddhahood, he
taught the Storehouse Teaching, also called the "Half-
word Teaching."[1] This is the Small Vehicle Teaching
aimed at the Sound Hearers. "But now," says the Buddha,
"I've spoken the Dharma right up to the very final
stage." THE TRUE AND REAL MUST BE SPOKEN/ I should reveal it all, without reservation. I should speak the
true, real Buddhadharma, to teach the real wisdom Bodhisattvas. It's not like before when I spoke the expedient
dharmas. I am speaking the real truth now. Previously I
said that if you have some small faults, it's all right.
You can gradually get rid of them. They aren't important.
It's okay. But now, you've really, really got to cultivate. You aren't allowed even the slightest fault. You
must work hard and be diligent in your cultivation. You

---

[1] 半字教 -pan tzu chiao.

must bring forth the heart of a Great Vehicle Bodhisattva. You can't be like you were before, stalling
around and procrastinating, putting off today's cultivation until tomorrow and tomorrow's until the day
after. That's being like the Venerable Ananda who
thought, "I am Shakyamuni Buddha's cousin. With a
Buddha for a cousin, I don't need to cultivate. He can
give me samadhi and spiritual powers." That was a real
mistake. In cultivation:

> You eat your own food, you fill yourself.
> You end your own birth and death.

To end birth and death, you must cultivate on your own.
No one can do it for you. They may say that they want to
help you, but that is just an expedient device to lead
you to resolve to cultivate on your own. If you don't
cultivate on your own, you won't end birth and death,
just as if someone else eats, you don't get full. You
must do it yourself. Put your feet firmly on the
ground and walk forward, step by step.

I TELL THE ASSEMBLY OF SOUND HEARERS/ The Buddha
previously taught the Dharma-door of the Four Holy
Truths to the Sound Hearers. AND THOSE WHO SEEK THE
CONDITIONED ENLIGHTENED VEHICLE/ The Buddha also taught
the Dharma of the Twelve Causes and Conditions   to the
Conditioned Enlightened Ones. THAT I WILL LEAD THEM TO
CAST OFF SUFFERING'S BOND/ With his compassionate heart,
the Buddha wants to cause all living beings to separate
from suffering and attain bliss, to end birth and cast
off death. They must understand that Impermanence comes
quickly. If you don't cultivate, but insist, "Wait a
minute. Slowly, slowly..." you had best be informed that
the ghost of Impermanence is not polite. When the time
comes for him to take you to see King Yama, he won't
show you the slightest bit of courtesy. If you try to
buy him off, to keep him away for awhile, and let you
live for a few more years, you can't do it. The Ghost
of Impermanence does not take bribes. He's not like
a greedy politician. In the world, with money, you can
do the impossible, If you break the law, but have the
cash, then "you didn't break the law." But the Ghost of
Impermanence has no greed in this regard. Money means
nothing to him. AND ARRIVE AT NIRVANA/ arrive at the
position of no-production and no extinction. THE BUDDHA
USES THE POWER OF EXPEDIENTS/ The Buddha uses the Dharma
of the Three Vehicles, the Sound Hearers, the Conditioned
Enlightened Ones, and the Bodhisattvas. DEMONSTRATING
THE THREE VEHICLE TEACHING/ He instructs in the Three
Vehicles for the sake of the One Buddha Vehicle. So, at

the very end, the Buddha speaks the Dharma of the One
Buddha Vehicle, the Dharma-door of real wisdom. SO THAT
LIVING BEINGS, ATTACHED IN MANY PLACES/ MAY BE GUIDED TO
ESCAPE/ Living beings, wherever they happen to be, get
attached in just that place. They get attached to whatever position they happen to be in. Fathers are
attached: "I am the father," they think, "and you are
my children," and they become attached. Older brothers
try to control their younger brothers. Why? Because
they are attached. They think, "I am the older brother
and you are the younger brother. You should listen to
my order." Husbands stand on a "husband platform,"
and wives stand on a "wife platform." Monks even stand
on a "monk platform," and novices stand on a "novice"
platform. "Look at me," they think, "I've left home and
you haven't!" That's an attachment.

People with learning are attached to learning. "I
am a professor and you are students. I should be your
teacher." That's also an attachment.

Students have student attachments. "I am a student
and if I don't know something, it's no problem. However,
since you are my teacher, if I ask you a question you
had better be able to answer it." However, in American
universities if the student asks a question and the
professor can't answer it, he just lets it go by; he
hasn't broken any laws.

In general, however, you have an attachment to
whatever you do. In the hells there are hellish attachments. Among the animals there are beastly attachments.
Among people there are human attachments. Among ghosts
there are ghostly attachments. That is why the text says,
"attached in many places." No matter where you are, no
matter what role you occupy, you will have precisely that
attachment. In a family, the older and younger brothers
and sisters, and the father and mother, and the grand-
parents all have their attachments. In the county
government--"I am the mayor and I have to manage the
officials. You have to listen to my orders. If you don't
I'm going to make it hard for you. I'll get in your way
and give you a bad time." These are all attachments.

The Buddhadharma was spoken just in order to
break the attachments of living beings. Once their
attachments have been destroyed, that is, if you have
no attachments, then the Buddhadharma is also ended; it
no longer exists. Why does the Buddhadharma exist? It is
just because you are attached. Without attachments, there
is no Buddhadharma. The Buddhadharma is for people with
attachments. When living beings no longer have attachments, the Buddhadharma is no longer of any use. Look-

ing at it that way, it would be best if living beings had a few more attachments! That way the Buddhadharma would be of some use. Otherwise, the Buddhadharma would "retire!"

The Buddha teaches living beings how to escape from their attachments, to become unattached. Without attachments, everyone would be happy and blissful.

Sutra: *(T.262,6a28)*

33-35At that time in the assembly there were Sound Hearers, Arhats with outflows extinguished, Ajnatakaundinya and others, twelve hundred persons, as well as Bhikshus, Bhikshunis, Upasakas, and Upasikas who had brought forth the resolve to become Sound Hearers and Pratyeka Buddhas. They all had the following thought:.36 "Why, now, does the World Honored One repeatedly praise the expedient devices saying, 'The Dharma obtained by the Buddha is so extremely profound and difficult to understand and the purport of his speech is so difficult to know, that none of the Sound Hearers or Pratyeka Buddhas can grasp it.' The Buddha has spoken of but one principle of liberation and we have already obtained this Dharma and arrived at Nirvana. Now, we do not understand his intention."

Commentary:

AT THAT TIME IN THE ASSEMBLY means when Shakyamuni Buddha had finished speaking the verses. This passage of text was added when the Sutra was compiled by the Venerable Ananda. Ananda said, "At that time, in the assembly, THERE WERE SOUND HEARERS, a vast number of those who had cultivated the Four Truths and awakened to the Way; they awoke to the Way upon hearing the Buddha's voice, and so their vehicle is called that of Sound Hearers. ARHATS WITH OUTFLOWS EXTINGUISHED. Their outflows had been exhausted. The exhaustion of outflows is called the Penetration of the Exhaustion of Outflows. Obtaining this penetration is the state of non-outflow, which means the absence of ignorance and affliction, as well as the absence of all bad habits and faults.

The presence of outflows may be likened to a bottle with a hole in it. You can keep pouring water in it, but it all runs out. People's bodies have many outflows.

But now, their outflows have been exhausted; all outflows have been ended and the Penetration of the Exhaustion of outflows has been attained.

"Arhat" is a Sanskrit word which means "worthy of offerings," "without birth," and "slayer of thieves."

At that time, among the Arhats, there was an elder by the name of AJNATAKAUNDINYA, also Sanskrit, which means "understanding the basic limit," or "the first to understand." After Shakyamuni Buddha realized Buddha-hood, he first went to the Deer Park to take Ajnata-kaundinya across. In a former life, Ajnatakaundinya was the King of Kalinga. Shakyamuni Buddha made a vow that when he became a Buddha the first person he would save would be the one who had cut his flesh from every limb. Therefore, after he became a Buddha, he first went to the Deer Park to take the five Bhikshus across. That's why Ajnata Kaundinya means, "the first to understand." He was the first to certify to the fruit of Arhatship. "Understanding the original limit" means that he under-stood his fundamental nature.

AND OTHERS, TWELVE HUNDRED PERSONS. Ajnatakaundinya had twelve hundred people with him.

AS WELL AS BHIKSHUS, BHIKSHUNIS, UPASAKAS, AND UPASIKAS WHO HAD BROUGHT FORTH THE RESOLVE TO BECOME SOUND HEARERS AND PRATYEKA BUDDHAS. There was another group that had resolved to seek the Vehicle of the Sound Hearers and Conditioned Enlightened Ones. As has been related many times before, the word Bhikshu has three meanings: "mendicant," "frightener of Mara," and "destroyer of evil." A Bhikshuni is a woman who has left home and the same three meanings apply. An Upasaka is a man closely related in affairs to the Sangha and and Upasika is a woman closely related in affairs to the Sangha. This means that they are lay people who draw near to the Triple Jewel.

WHO ALL HAD THE FOLLOWING THOUGHT: Each of them had this thought.

What did they think?

"WHY, NOW, at present, DOES THE WORLD HONORED ONE, Shakyamuni Buddha, REPEATEDLY PRAISE THE EXPEDIENT DEVICES?" He praises it again and again. The term here which is rendered "repeatedly" usually means "diligently."[1] Here, however, it means that the Buddha

---

[1] 殷勤 -yin ch'in.

is not lazy in speaking the Sutra. He speaks it once and yet again, and praises it once and yet again. First, he praises it in prose and then he repeats his praise in verse, and when he speaks the doctrine he takes it very seriously. He is not the least bit sloppy because it is very important and it is to be feared that people won't pay attention unless he very seriously praises the expedient devices and does so repeatedly.

SAYING, 'THE DHARMA OBTAINED BY THE BUDDHA,' the Dharma which I, Shakyamuni Buddha, have obtained IS SO EXTREMELY PROFOUND AND DIFFICULT TO UNDERSTAND. No one knows how deep it is; thus it is extremely profound. No one can understand it; thus it is hard to understand. AND THE PURPORT OF HIS SPEECH IS SO DIFFICULT TO KNOW. The meaning of what the Buddha says is not easy to understand. THAT NONE OF THE SOUND HEARERS OR PRATYEKA BUDDHAS CAN GRASP IT. Those of the Two Vehicles cannot understand this doctrine.

THE BUDDHA HAS SPOKEN BUT ONE PRINCIPLE OF LIBERATION AND WE HAVE ALREADY OBTAINED THIS DHARMA AND REACHED NIRVANA. We of the Sound Hearer Vehicle have completely attained the doctrine of the principle of liberation and rely on it to cultivate. We have already gained the bliss of Nirvana. NOW, WE DO NOT UNDERSTAND HIS INTENTION." The Buddha now says that his previous teaching was not ultimate, not final. It was not true and real. You have lectured us all into a daze and we don't know what this means. Ultimately, what is the principle? What is the Buddha's intention? We've already got doubts. The Dharmas the Buddha spoke previously--were they incorrect? Then is what he is now saying correct? Even though they were incorrect, they still brought us advantages. We managed to certify to the first, second, third, and fourth stages of Arhatship. Now, if that's incorrect, then most likely the fruits we have certified to are false as well.

Everyone has doubts.

Sutra: (T.262,6b7)

37-40 At that time Shariputra, knowing the doubts in the minds of the four-fold assembly, and himself not yet fully understanding, addressed the Buddha saying, "For what reason has the World Honored One repeatedly praised the foremost expedient devices of the Buddhas and the extremely profound and wonderful Dharma which is difficult to understand?[41] From the past onwards I have never heard

the Buddha speak in such a way. Presently, the four-fold assembly
all has doubts. I only pray that the World Honored One will
expound upon this subject: Why has the World Honored One re-
peatedley praised the Dharma which is extremely profound, subtle,
and hard to understand?"

Commentary:

AT THAT TIME, when the four-fold assembly started
to have doubts, the wisest of the Sound Hearers, SHARI-
PUTRA, KNOWING THE DOUBTS IN THE MINDS OF THE FOUR-FOLD
ASSEMBLY...He knew that all the disciples had doubts and
that their minds were confused and muddled. But although
he was so intelligent and wise, he didn't understand the
state of the Buddha either. So the text says, AND HIM-
SELF NOT YET FULLY UNDERSTANDING. He ADDRESSED THE
BUDDHA, SAYING, "FOR WHAT REASON HAS THE WORLD HONORED
ONE REPEATEDLY PRAISED THE FOREMOST EXPEDIENT DHARMAS OF
THE BUDDHAS in such a way repeatedly extolling and laud-
ing them, praising the foremost expedient devices AND
THE EXTREMELY PROFOUND AND WONDERFUL DHARMA WHICH IS SO
HARD TO UNDERSTAND?" It is so deep, so fine and subtle,
so hard to understand, this wonderful Dharma of real
wisdom.
    "FROM THE PAST ONWARDS...I have been following
Shakyamuni Buddha now for over forty years. It took
eight years to speak *The Dharma Flower Sutra* and one day
and one night to speak *The Mahaparinirvana Sutra*. If you
spread the palm leaves which they were written on out
end to end, they would stretch across a distance of
eight miles.
    Shariputra had been with the Buddha for over forty
years and he had doubts. When the Buddha was in the
world, some of his disciples believed in him, some had
doubts. However, they all wanted to study the Buddhadharma. They listened to the Buddha speak the Sutras
and they cultivated under him. They never left him.
That is why the twelve hundred and fifty disciples are
called his "constant retinue." In every Dharma assembly,
Shakyamuni Buddha always had at the very least twelve
hundred and fifty people as an audience. Even if they
didn't understand the doctrines he was explaining, they
still investigated the Buddhadharma and came to listen.
So the text says, "From the past onwards." The word
"past" tells us that Shariputra had been with the
Buddha and never left him. He listened to the Buddhadharma every day and studied it every day.

"I HAVE NEVER HEARD THE BUDDHA SPEAK IN SUCH A WAY. When you spoke the Dharma before, you never said such important things. PRESENTLY, THE FOUR-FOLD ASSEMBLY ALL HAS DOUBTS. The entire assembly of disciples has given rise to doubts. They don't know where their confusion came from and they don't know where it's going. They don't know where to begin, which Dharma-door to cultivate. This is a serious problem and so I ONLY PRAY THAT THE WORLD HONORED ONE WILL EXPOUND UPON THIS SUBJECT and elucidate this matter in fine detail to clear up the doubts of those present here. Please don't leave us, as it were, standing at the fork in the road not knowing which way to turn. WHY HAS THE WORLD HONORED ONE RE-PEATEDLY PRAISED THE DHARMA WHICH IS EXTREMELY PROFOUND, SUBTLE, AND HARD TO UNDERSTAND? Why? We don't understand and so we ask the Buddha to be compassionate and instruct us. We respectfully await the holy instruction."

Sutra: (T.262,6b14)

42-43 At that time, Shariputra, wishing to restate

this meaning, spoke verses saying,

> O, Sun of Wisdom, Great Honored Sage,
>
> Long have you waited to speak this Dharma;

Commentary:

What is meant by the SUN OF WISDOM? In this world, the light of the Buddha's wisdom is like the light of the sun.

GREAT HONORED SAGE: The Buddha is the god among the gods, the sage among the sages. Thus, he is called the Great Honored Sage. Before the Buddha appeared in the world, the world was without the Buddhadharma. A world without the Buddhadharma is like a world without a sun. Without the sun, in the midst of night, we are in dark-ness. When the Buddha appeared in the world, in was as if the sun had ascended into space, dispersing all dark-ness with its light.

What does this mean?

Before the Buddha appeared in the world, the world was without true principle. It wasn't that true principle didn't exist, but rather that no one understood it. True principle, of course, neither comes nor goes. However, if no one points it out, people who have been sunk in con-fusion for so long will not perceive it.

What is the confusion that people are sunk in?

The five desires: forms, sounds, smells, tastes, and tangible objects. These are the objects of the five senses, also called the five desires.

Form: No one is able to see through and break their attachment to forms. People are attached to forms. Anything with shape and appearance is considered form, but among such shapes and appearances people select the good ones. People don't like the bad. They pick beautiful forms. Because they enjoy them so much, they sink, drunk with the objects of form.

Sounds: People like to listen to music, to singing, and perhaps even to the chirping of birds and the sounds of people talking in pleasant tones. This is to sink and drown in the objects of sound, drunk on the defiling dust of sound.

Smells: people also covet smells. If you eat one kind of food, you might smell another kind of food cooking and decide that you want it instead. After eating the other kind for a while, another aromatic dish may catch your attention and you will want to eat that. It's like being drunk on wine, sunk in the confusion of the defiling objects of smell.

Tastes: Today you may want to eat fish, tomorrow chicken, and the day after duck or beef. But when you are eating beef, you think that it's not as tasty as lamb. Whatever is hardest to come by is just what you think would be the very best. Things you've eaten, you tire of. This is because of greed and desire. To be caught up in the desire for food and sink into the stupor created by objects of taste is like being caught in quicksand. You just get one leg out and the other sinks in deeper. You never get out of the quicksand. So it is with the object of taste.

Tangible objects: People like to come in contact with all manner of smooth surfaces. They like to wear silk and satin fabrics which not only protect their skin but are soft and warm as well. Men and women become attached to each other as objects of touch and so sink into the stupor caused by defiling tangible objects as if stuck in quicksand unable to get their legs free. They just get one leg out and the other leg sinks right in.

Thus, people are unable to extricate themselves from the realms of the five desires.

Those of outside ways use the five desires in their teachings, and they don't lead living beings to break free of their attachments. Therefore, they live in a dark night, sunk in confusion, in a stupor, in a state of dream-like confusion, and the entire world is pitch black. When the Buddha appeared in the world, it was as though the sun had started to shine. People were taught not to be attached to the five desires, the defiling objects of sense. So the text says, "O Sun of Wisdom, Great Honored Sage."

LONG HAVE YOU WAITED TO SPEAK THIS DHARMA/ "Long" means that he never spoke it before. Shakyamuni Buddha had been speaking the Dharma for a long time, but it was always the provisional Dharma. It was provisional wisdom. He has never spoken the real wisdom. Now, at the very end, the genuine real wisdom is being spoken for everyone to hear.

Sutra:(T.262, 6b15)

> Speaking of your attainments of such
>
> Powers, fearlessnesses, and samadhis,
>
> Dhyana samadhis and liberations,
>
> And other inconceivable dharmas.

Commentary:

Shakyamuni Buddha spoke the Dharma for forty-nine years in over three hundred assemblies and from the very beginning right through to the end, he never spoke the real; he only spoke the provisional . Here, in the Lotus Assembly, he finally speaks the real wisdom. SPEAKING OF YOUR ATTAINMENTS OF SUCH/ POWERS, FEARLESS-NESSES, AND SAMADHIS/ There are Ten Powers and Four Fearlessnesses. DHYANA SAMADHIS AND LIBERATIONS/ There are Eight Liberations, also called "Eight Renunciations off the Back." AND OTHER INCONCEIVABLE DHARMAS/ These Dharmas cannot be thought about with the mind or expressed in words.

Sutra: (T.262,6b17)

> Concerning the Dharma attained in the Bodhimanda,
>
> No one is able to raise a question.
>
> I find its meaning hard to fathom,
>
> And am also unable to ask about it.
>
> So you speak unasked,
>
> Praising the path you have walked
>
> And that wisdom fine and subtle,
> Attained by all the Buddhas.

44

    All the Arhats, without outflows,

    And those who seek Nirvana,

    Have fallen into a net of doubts.

  "Why has the Buddha said this?"

    Those who seek Condition Enlightenment,

    The Bhikshus, the Bhikshunis,

    Gods, dragons, ghosts, and spirits,

    Gandharvas and others,

    Look at one another, perplexed,

    And then gaze at the Doubly Complete Honored One.

  "What is the meaning of this matter?

  "We pray that the Buddha will explain."

Commentary:

CONCERNING THE DHARMA OBTAINED IN THE BODHIMANDA/ the fine and subtle Dharma the Buddha obtained in the Bodhimanda. NO ONE IS ABLE TO RAISE A QUESTION/ We don't know how to approach the subject because it is real wisdom, not the provisional wisdom of the Sound Hearers. Those of the Three Vehicles can't even ask about it. I FIND ITS MEANING HARD TO FATHOM/ AND AM ALSO UNABLE TO ASK ABOUT IT/ Because no one understands it, no one is able to ask about it.

SO YOU SPEAK UNASKED/ PRAISING THE PATH YOU HAVE WALKED/ AND THAT WISDOM, FINE AND SUBTLE/ ATTAINED BY ALL THE BUDDHAS/ You praise the true, real wisdom, the extremely profound wisdom which is understood only by all the Buddhas in the ten directions and by Shakyamuni Buddha.

ALL THE ARHATS, WITHOUT OUTFLOWS/ Although they have ended outflows and are Fourth Stage Arhats, AND THOSE WHO SEEK NIRVANA/ or they are Bodhisattvas of the Provisional Vehicle who seek Nirvana, or perhaps they are Pratyeka Buddhas HAVE FALLEN INTO A NET OF DOUBTS/ Hearing the Buddha speak of the true, real wisdom which is extremely profound, subtle, and wonderful, rare and foremost, everyone has doubts; they have fallen into a net of doubt. If one has doubts, one can't cultivate the Way. As I have often said before,

        Cultivators of the Way

           take care not to doubt.

                    Once doubt arises
                        it's easy to get lost.
If you have doubts, you will lose your way.   So now, the
Sound Hearers, the Conditioned Enlightened Ones, and
the Provisional Teaching Bodhisattvas--every last one
of them--have fallen into the net of doubts.

        "WHY HAS THE BUDDHA SAID THIS?"/ Why has he
spoken such a frightening dharma? It has caused everyone to have fox-like doubts and to disbelieve, to be
frightened and alarmed.

        THOSE WHO SEEK CONDITIONED ENLIGHTENMENT/
THE BHIKSHUS, THE BHIKSHUNIS/ GODS, DRAGONS, GHOSTS
AND SPIRITS/ GANDHARVAS AND OTHERS/ LOOK AT ONE ANOTHER
PERPLEXED/ Everyone stares at everyone else. You look
at me and I look at you and nobody understands what's
going on. "Perplexed" means that they have doubts which
have not been resolved. In their hearts, they don't
know what would be best. Should they go south or should
they go north or should they go east or west? They've
gotten to the intersection but they don't know which
road to take. There they stand in the middle of the
street, not knowing which way to go. They are perplexed. AND THEN GAZE AT THE DOUBLY COMPLETE HONORED
ONE/ They stare fixedly at the Buddha, not turning
their gaze away for a moment. They stare up at him,
because he is sitting high upon the Dharma-seat. They
all tilt their heads back to gaze at him.

        What is meant by the "Doubly Complete Honored
One?"It means that the Buddha is complete in both
blessings and wisdom. This is because he cultivated
blessings and wisdom for three asankhyeya aeons and
perfected the fine marks for a hundred aeons. There
are eighty fine marks.

        One cultivates blessings by making offerings to
the Triple Jewel, by drawing near to all the Buddhas,
by making offerings to the Buddha, the Dharma, and
the Sangha, to the Bodhisattvas, Pratyeka Buddhas, and
Arhats. For three great uncountable aeons, the Buddha
vastly cultivated the practice of making offerings.
He didn't make offerings to just one Buddha, but to
very many of them.

        One cultivates wisdom, first of all, by holding
the precepts. Why? If one holds the precepts, one can
give rise to samadhi. From samadhi, comes wisdom. If
you have samadhi power, you will have wisdom power.

        What is samadhi power?

        Samadhi power means not being turned by any ex-
ternal states. Neither good nor bad can move your mind.
Whether the situation that arises is favorable or con-

trary, your heart does not move. If you can have an un-
moving mind, you will have samadhi power. Once you have
samadhi power, then you can have wisdom power.

Shakyamuni Buddha cultivated blessings and wisdom.
One cultivates wisdom by studying the Sutras; the
Study of the Sutras augments one's wisdom. If you do not
Study the Sutras, you won't be able to increase your
wisdom. If your wisdom is not increasing, it is de-
creasing. Therefore, you must study all of the Sutras,
Shastras, and the Vinaya. Study the Tripitaka diligently;
that's cultivating wisdom.

If you only cultivate blessings and do not cultivate wisdom, what kind of fruit will you reap?

One who cultivates blessings and not wisdom
Is like an elephant wearing a necklace.

In the future you'll be a big elephant, tall and strong,
wearing a fine necklace. You'll look striking enough,
but you won't have any wisdom or intelligence.

One who cultivates wisdom and not blessings,
Is like and Arhat with an empty bowl.

If you just study the Sutras but do not do good deeds
or plant good roots...

But how does one plant good roots?
Just by doing good deeds!

Not doing any evil &
Doing many good deeds.

This is to plant and tend your good roots. If you
merely study Sutras and never do good deeds or help
other people, you'll be like the Arhat with an empty
begging bowl. You may certify to the fruit of Arhatship, but when you go out to beg no one will make offerings to you. "So you've certified to the fruit?" they
will say. "So what?" No one will make offerings to you
because you did not cultivate blessings in the causal
ground and so you have no blessings now.

I often tell you these two sentences:
To endure suffering is to end suffering.
To ejoy blessings brings an end to blessings.

You suffer? Why do you suffer? It's because in
previous lifetimes you did not cultivate blessings and
so you must endure bitterness now. If you can endure
your present suffering, it will pass. If you don't undergo that suffering which you deserve, it will remain
latent. If you take what you deserve, it will disappear.

If you have a bit of blessed retribution but you
just spend your days enjoying yourself, living in a
nice house, eating good food, buying fine furnishings,
the latest model car, or even your own airplane so that

you can fly around as you please, and you do not take
even the least bit of suffering, you use up your blessings. Once they've been used up, you won't have any more.
Once you've enjoyed all your happiness, you will have
to undergo suffering. Do you know how much happiness you
have coming to you? If you enjoy it all, you'll end up
suffering again.

Shakyamuni Buddha cultivated both blessings and
wisdom, and so he is called the Doubly Complete Honored One, complete in blessings and wisdom.

"WHAT IS THE MEANING OF THIS MATTER?"/ They
stare unblinking at the World Honored One, and in
their hearts they hope that the Buddha will explain in
detail the meaning of his praising the wonderful Dharma.
"WE PRAY THAT THE BUDDHA WILL EXPLAIN.?"/ All of us
ask the Buddha to tell us in detail the principles involved here, the meaning behind all of this.

Sutra: (T.262,6b27)

45 Of the host of Sound Hearers

The Buddha has declared me foremost,

And yet now with my own wisdom

I cannot resolve my doubts.

Is this Dharma ultimate?

Or is it the path to be walked?

46 Disciples born from the Buddha's mouth,

With joined palms wait, expectantly.

Pray put forth the subtle sound,

For it's time to tell it as it really is.

47 The gods, dragons, spirits, and others

Their numbers like the Ganges' sands,

Bodhisattvas seeking Buddhahood,

Numbering a full eighty thousand,

And, from myriads of millions of lands,

Wheel-Turning Sage Kings have come,

With joined palms and reverent minds

All wish to hear of the perfect way.

Commentary:

OF THE HOST OF SOUND HEARERS/ In the assembly of
Shravakas, THE BUDDHA HAS DECLARED ME FOREMOST/ The
World Honored One has said that I, Shariputra, am
number one in wisdom. He says that I'm the smartest!
AND YET NOW WITH MY OWN WISDOM/ However, presently, I
myself, thinking it over with my number one wisdom
I CANNOT RESOLVE MY DOUBTS/ I'm all confused. Although
I'm number one in wisdom, I'm not living up to my
position. Why? Because I don't *get it*, that's why! I've
given rise to doubts, and so as number one, I'm all
washed up.
IS THIS DHARMA ULTIMATE?/ Is this the ultimate,
subtle, wonderful, extremely deep Dharma, OR IS IT THE
PATH TO BE WALKED?/ Or is it the perfect, subtle, and
wonderful Way of Bodhi which the Thus Come One culti-
vated?
DISCIPLES, BORN FROM THE BUDDHA'S MOUTH/ All of the
Bodhisattvas are disciples of the Dharma King. They are
the Buddha's true children. They are
Born from the Buddha's mouth,
Transformed from the Dharma.
That's why the text says, "Disciples, born from the
Buddha's mouth." WITH JOINED PALMS WAIT, EXPECTANTLY/
We place our palms together and gaze at the Buddha, wait-
ing for him to speak this deep Dharma of real wisdom.
PRAY PUT FORTH THE WONDROUS SOUND/ We all want the
World Honored One to put forth the sound of Dharma FOR
IT'S TIME TO TELL IT AS IT REALLY IS/ Explain the true,
real doctrine.
THE GODS, DRAGONS, SPIRITS AND OTHERS/ All the gods
in the heavens, and the dragons, and so on and the
entire eight-fold division THEIR NUMBER LIKE THE GANGES'
SANDS/ So many of them! BODHISATTVAS SEEKING BUDDHAHOOD/
NUMBERING A FULLY EIGHTY THOUSAND/ AND, FROM MYRIADS OF
MILLIONS OF LANDS/ WHEEL-TURNING SAGE KINGS HAVE COME/
There are Gold Wheel-Turning Kings, Silver, Copper, and
Iron Wheel-Turning Kings--all four categories of Wheel-
Turning Kings came. WITH JOINED PALMS AND REVERENT MINDS/
They have placed their palms together most repectfully
because they ALL WISH TO HEAR OF THE PERFECT WAY/ They
all want to hear about that wonderful Dharma-door the
World Honored One cultivated and that perfect, complete
Bodhi Way he attained.

Sutra: (T.262,6c7)

48At that time the Buddha told Shariputra, "Stop! Stop! There
is no need to speak further. If this matter were spoken of, the
gods and humans in all the worlds would be frightened and led to
doubt."

49 Shariputra again addressed the Buddha saying, "World Honored
One, I only pray that you will speak it. I only pray that you will
speak it. What is the reason? In this assembly are countless
hundreds of thousands of myriads of millions of asankhyeyas of
living beings who have, in the past, seen the Buddhas. Their roots
are keen and their wisdom bright. Hearing what the Buddha says
they will be able to revere and believe it."

At that time, Shariputra, wishing to restate this meaning,
spoke the following verses:

Dharma King, Supremely Honored One,

Do but speak; pray have no worries,

For, within the limitless multitudes,

Are those who can revere and believe it.

Commentary:

AT THAT TIME, when Shariputra had requested the
Buddha to speak the Dharma THE BUDDHA TOLD SHARIPUTRA,
"STOP! It can't be spoken; it should not be spoken. It
is ineffable, ineffable. STOP!" He said it twice." Don't
talk about this Dharma." Why not?
THERE IS NO NEED TO SPEAK FURTHER. Say, let's not
talk about this Dharma. Just forget it, okay? IF THIS
MATTER WERE SPOKEN OF, that is, if I spoke the Dharma
of true reality, the real wisdom Dharma, the ultimate
Dharma THE GODS AND HUMANS IN ALL THE WORLDS WOULD BE
FRIGHTENED AND LED TO DOUBT. Why? If you speak to them
of expedient devices, the provisional dharmas, they can
accept them. If you tell them the real Dharma, they won't
believe it. People all have this quirk: When you lie to
them, they usually believe you, but when you tell them
the truth, they don't believe you. If you tell them,
"You shouldn't have desire. You shouldn't entertain
thoughts of sexual desire," they are bound to doubt you.
"I don't know if that's really the case," they will

say. "I mean, really, what's the point of having no
sexual desire?" They think such behaviour is extremely
blissful. "What do you mean that if you cultivate you
can't indulge in such activities?"

And so some people call themselves Buddhists, but
they do not teach people to cut off their thoughts of
sexual desire. They cheat themselves and they cheat
others. If the Buddhadharma rests with people like
this, then it has truly become extinct.

It's really pathetic. If you tell people the
truth, they are afraid and they don't believe you. Not
only do they disbelieve, but they slander you as well.
"Hah!" they say, "He doesn't understand the Buddhadharma. He just speaks confusedly."

SHARIPUTRA AGAIN ADDRESSED THE BUDDHA, SAYING,
Shakyamuni Buddha had decided not to speak the Dharma;
he was not going to expound *The Dharma Flower Sutra*.
Shariputra begged him to speak, however.

Basically, before speaking the Sutras, the Dharma
should be requested. But in a country where there is no
Buddhadharma, you can't really wait around for someone
to ask. I waited for five or six years. The chance
didn't come until the summer of 1968 when all of you
Americans came here to study the Buddhadharma. At that
time I quit waiting and started speaking.

Now, the Buddha won't speak. He says, "Stop! I'm
not going to speak. Stop! I'm not going to talk." On
the other hand, I say, "Don't stop! I'm going to speak.
I'm going to speak every day." Recently, I said to a
Tibetan who visited, "The students of the Dharma here
have obtained a taste of the Dharma's sweetness and
so they don't want to quit. I, myself, find it extremely
bitter. Why? I have to lecture every day and, on top of
that, I don't even get paid! Hah! In China when people
lecture on the Sutras, say on *The Dharma Flower Sutra*, they
make a lot of money. Of course, I am just joking.

WORLD HONORED ONE, I ONLY PRAY THAT YOU WILL
SPEAK IT. He calls out, "World Honored One, please,
please won't you speak it? I ONLY PRAY THAT YOU WILL
SPEAK IT." This shows his extreme sincerity. He has
now asked twice.

WHAT IS THE REASON? Why do I ask the Buddha to
speak this Dharma? IN THIS ASSEMBLY ARE COUNTLESS
HUNDREDS OF THOUSANDS OF MYRIADS OF MILLIONS OF
ASANKHYEYAS OF LIVING BEINGS, that's a lot! WHO HAVE IN
THE PAST, SEEN THE BUDDHAS. In the past they saw the
Buddhas and in the present they see the World Honored
One. THEIR ROOTS ARE KEEN AND THEIR WISDOM BRIGHT. They
are very intelligent because, in the past, they planted

many good roots. HEARING WHAT THE BUDDHA SAYS, THEY
WILL BE ABLE TO REVERE AND BELIEVE IT. When they hear
Shakyamuni Buddha say it, they will believe it. Please,
Buddha, be compassionate and expound this extremely
deep, subtle and wonderful Dharma.

AT THAT TIME,SHARIPUTRA, WISHING TO RESTATE THIS
MEANING, SPOKE THE FOLLOWING VERSES:

DHARMA KING, SUPREMELY HONORED ONE/ In the world
and beyond the world, there is no one higher than you.
I again ask you to speak this wonderful Dharma. DO BUT
SPEAK; PRAY HAVE NO WORRIES/ Don't have any second
thoughts. Don't be concerned that people might not be-
live what you say. FOR, WITHIN THE LIMITLESS MULTITUDES/
ARE THOSE WHO CAN REVERE AND BELIEVE IT/ There most
certainly be those who will respect and have faith in
this Dharma and who will not become doubtful.

Sutra: (T.262,6c16)

50 The Buddha again stopped Shariputra, "If this matter were

spoken of, the gods, humans, and asuras in all the worlds would

be frightened and led to doubt, and those Bhikshus of overweening

pride would fall into a big pit."

Then the World Honored One restated his meaning in verse,

saying,

> Stop, stop. It must not be spoken.
>
> My Dharma is wonderful beyond conception,
>
> And those of undue pride who heard it,
>
> Surely would neither revere or believe it.

Commentary:

THE BUDDHA AGAIN STOPPED SHARIPUTRA, SAYING, The
Buddha had already said "Stop," twice before. This is
his third refusal. He said, "There's no need to speak
about it. Why not? "IF THIS MATTER WERE SPOKEN OF, THE
GODS, HUMANS, AND ASURAS IN ALL THE WORLDS WOULD BE
FRIGHTENED AND LED TO DOUBT, AND THOSE BHIKSHUS OF
OVERWEENING PRIDE WOULD FALL INTO A BIG PIT." The
Bhikshus are arrogant and self-satisfied. Why? Because
they have attachments, that's why. They are attached to
the opinion that no one is equal to them, and so they
are going to fall into a great big trap. They think they
are clever and that their intelligence and conduct far

surpass everyone else's.

Once people become slightly intelligent, not greatly wise, by any means, they tend to expose it wherever they go. They shine their light outwardly to show off that they are number one; they are unable to contain their light within themselves. If you have a lot of light, that means that you are intelligent but you don't display your intelligence. You keep it covered and hidden away.

"Well, isn't that just being greedy?" you ask.

No. It's wanting to avoid becoming arrogant and proud.

Arrogance is the attitude that "I am better than everyone else." For example, "I am an Oriental and they are the very best. The yellow race is the most superior in the world." That is arrogance. Someone else might think, "I am Caucasian, and the white race is the best. We are the most intelligent." That is also arrogance.

One may be a Negro who thinks that the white and yellow races are inferior and that the black people are the most superior. That, too, is arrogance. Regardless of whether or not you are white, yellow, black, red, or green, no matter what race you are or what kind of person you are, you should not hold the view of arrogance. In China there is a saying,

> Modesty brings benefits,
> But arrogance causes harm.

It is because of your arrogance that you keep hitting your head against the wall and are unable to study and learn from others. Arrogance is an obstacle to your learning. You can't learn if your mind is filled with self-pride, because you think you already know everything. "What have I got to learn?" you think.

Those who study the Buddhadharma should not master one tiny bit of it and then think, "I know it all!"

What do you know? And those who have not studied the Buddhadharma have even less business being arrogant. It's really pathetic. They don't understand anything at all, but they become arrogant.

For example, last summer one of my disciples said that since he was a "special person" he didn't have to study the Shurangama Mantra. When he left home I gave him seven days to learn it, and then extended the seven days to fourteen, but he still could not learn it. Now, he can probably recite it, but I was very strict with him because he was fairly sincere. Why was he unable to learn it? Because he was arrogant in thinking that he was "special" and did not need to study it. But just wait until the time comes when he needs to use it!

Arrogant people have a kind of power. They can read and remember Sutras at a fast rate. Whatever they do, they do very perfectly because they are smarter and quicker than others. Because of this, they get arrogant. They can do things better and faster than others. They study the Sutras fast, they study the Dharma fast, the cultivate and become Buddhas fast, they enter samadhi and give rise to wisdom fast. But take care not to become attached to a view of self and think that you are better than others. Don't put yourself on a pedastal.

The Bhikshus of overweening pride are in for a suprise. They are going to fall into a big pit. They figure they know everything and so when they hear the real Dharma, they won't believe it. Because they fail to believe, they will fall into the pit, a very low place. The "big pit" refers to the three evil paths, the hells, the animal realm, and the realm of the hungry ghosts.

AT THAT TIME THE WORLD HONORED ONE RESTATED HIS MEANING IN VERSE, SAYING, "STOP,STOP. IT MUST NOT BE SPOKEN/ MY DHARMA IS WONDERFUL BEYOND CONCEPTION/ Because this Dharma is so subtle and wonderful, it is not easy to think about, not easy to believe. If the Buddha spoke this true, real Dharma, no one would believe it. AND THOSE OF UNDUE PRIDE WHO HEARD IT/ the arrogant Bhikshus SURELY WOULD NEITHER REVERE OR BELIEVE IT/ They wouldn't understand it. They wouldn't believe it. They wouldn't revere it.

Sutra: (T.262,6c21)
   51

At that time, Shariputra further addressed the Buddha, saying, "World Honored One, I only pray that you will speak it; I only pray that you will speak it. Presently, within this assembly are those who are my equal, hundreds of thousands of myriads of millions of them. Life after life they have been transformed by the Buddha. People such as these will surely be able to revere and believe you. They will gain security and great benefit within the long night."

At that time, Shariputra, wishing to restate his meaning, recited the following verses:

Supreme and Doubly Honored One.

Pray speak the foremost Dharma.

I, the Buddha's eldest disciple,

Wish you will but speak it in detail.

The limitless host here assembled,

Can revere and believe this Dharma,

For the Buddha has, for life after life,

Taught and transformed such ones as these.

With one mind, with palms joined,

We all wish to hear the Buddha speak.

Twelve hundred of us there are,

And more, seeking Buddhahood.

Pray, for those assembled here,

Speak of it in detail;

Having heard this Dharma,

Great will our rejoicing be.

Commentary:

AT THAT TIME, after Shariputra had heard the Buddha speak the previous verse, SHARIPUTRA FURTHER ADDRESSED THE BUDDHA, SAYING, with earnest faith, I ONLY PRAY THAT YOU WILL SPEAK IT; I ONLY PRAY THAT YOU WILL SPEAK IT. With firm faith I know that PRESENTLY, WITHIN THIS ASSEMBLY ARE THOSE WHO ARE MY EQUAL. Like me, their faith is also firm and they wish the Buddha will speak this extremely deep and wonderful Dharma. "Those who are my equal" refers to those of the same rank, the Bhikshus, Bhikshunis, Upasakas, and Upasikas. HUNDREDS OF THOUSANDS OF MYRIADS OF MILLIONS OF THEM. LIFE AFTER LIFE, THEY HAVE BEEN TRANSFORMED BY THE BUDDHA. For a long time, these people have received the Buddha's instruction and teaching. Those who haven't received the teaching of the Buddha in the past will not believe the Buddhadharma when they hear it. If they have already received the teaching in the past, for many lives, then they will believe it right when they hear it and feel sure that it is something they can have faith in. The Buddha has many disciples because, life after life, he has taught and transformed sentient beings. The sentient beings also vowed, life after life, to follow the Buddha and study the Buddhadharma. When the Buddha was a Bhikshu, these people all took refuge with the Triple Jewel. When the Buddha gained the first stage of Arhatship, they left

home. When the Buddha became a second stage Arhat, they
followed him to cultivate the Way. Shakyamuni Buddha
used the great compassion heart and many expedient devices to teach and transform his disciples. When the
Buddha accomplished the fruit of Buddhahood, they all
became Arhats because through successive lives they had
received the Buddha's teaching.

In this life, since Shakyamuni Buddha has already
become a Buddha, we are becoming Bhikshus. Such causal
affinities develop as, life after life, we receive the
merciful and compassionate instruction of the Buddha.

PEOPLE SUCH AS THESE WILL SURELY BE ABLE TO REVERE
AND BELIEVE YOU. No matter what doctrines the Buddha
speaks, they will believe him. THEY WILL GAIN SECURITY
AND GREAT BENEFIT WITHIN THE LONG NIGHT of time. We are
dreaming and in our sleep know nothing. Shakyamuni
Buddha, you should speak this wonderful Dharma. Have
pity on us. Speak the Dharma so we may gain great advantage.

When I was in Manchuria and Hong Kong, my disciples
had great faith in me. No matter what I said, they believed it, and they had no doubts whatsoever. Even when
I deliberately said something contrary to the doctrine,
they still believed it. Those who had taken refuge for
the first time did not have such firm faith. Those who
had taken refuge for two, three, four, or five lifetimes didn't have such firm faith; but other others did.
So, Shakyamuni Buddha had taught and transformed these
people throughout many lives.

Shariputra has asked the Buddha to speak the wonderful doctrine and said that everyone would certainly
be able to believe it.Even though he said that, still,
later on, five thousand Bhikshus, Bhikshunis, Upasakas
and Upasikas got up and walked out. Shakyamuni Buddha
is just about to speak the wonderful Dharma, and he says
that he will explain it in great detail and five thousand
people walk out. This can be compared to threshing rice.
When you toss the rice high into the air, the wind
blows the chaff away, and the rice grains fall down.
The five thousand who left are like the chaff.

AT THAT TIME, SHARIPUTRA, WISHING TO RESTATE THIS
MEANING SPOKE VERSES, SAYING, "SUPREME AND DOUBLY HONORED
ONE/ "Supreme" means that there is no one higher.
"Doubly Honored" means that the Buddha is complete in
both blessings and wisdom. PRAY SPEAK THE FOREMOST DHARMA/
We wish you to speak the true, wonderful, real Dharma-
door which is number one, without a number two. I, THE
BUDDHA'S ELDEST DISCIPLE/ I, Shariputra, am the Buddha's
eldest disciple, WISH YOU WILL BUT SPEAK IT IN DETAIL/

I hope the Buddha will be compassionate and speak this Dharma to me. THE LIMITLESS HOST HERE ASSEMBLED/ CAN REVERE AND BELIEVE THIS DHARMA/ Why are they able to believe it? FOR THE BUDDHA HAS, LIFE AFTER LIFE/TAUGHT AND TRANSFORMED SUCH ONES AS THESE/Because they have received the compassionate teaching of the Buddha and the nourishment of the milk of Dharma, they revere and believe it. WITH ONE MIND, WITH PALMS JOINED/ WE ALL WISH TO HEAR THE BUDDHA SPEAK/ TWELVE HUNDRED OF US THERE ARE/ AND MORE, SEEKING BUDDHAHOOD/ There are Pratyeka Buddhas and Provisional Teaching Bodhisattvas. PRAY, FOR THOSE ASSEMBLED HERE/ SPEAK OF IT IN DETAIL/ FOR HAVING HEARD THIS DHARMA/ GREAT WILL OUR REJOICING BE/ Please be compassionate and speak to us. We will certainly rejoice."

Sutra: (T.262,7a5)

52-57 Thereupon the World Honored One told Shariputra, "Since you have earnestly requested three times, how can I not speak? [58] You should now listen attentively, think upon it well, and be mindful of it; I will explain it in detail for your sake."

[59] As he said these words, five thousand Bhikshus, Bhikshunis, Upasakas, and Upasikas in the assembly rose from their seats, made obeisance to the Buddha and left. What was the reason? The roots of their offenses were deep and grave and they were of such overweening pride that they claimed to have obtained what they had not yet obtained and to have certified to that to which they had not yet certified to. With faults such as these they could not stay. The World Honored One remained silent and did not restrain them.

The Buddha then told Shariputra, "My assembly has now been cleared of its branches and leaves and only the trunks remain. Shariputra, it is excellent that those of overweening pride have left. You should now listen well and I shall speak it for you."

[60] Shariputra said, "So be it, World Honored One. I wish joyfully to hear it."

Commentary:

THEREUPON THE WORLD HONORED ONE   TOLD   SHARIPUTRA,

"SINCE YOU HAVE EARNESTLY REQUESTED **THREE TIMES**, HOW
COULD I NOT SPEAK?" You have repeated your request
three times; how could I refuse to speak this Dharma to
you? YOU SHOULD NOW LISTEN ATTENTIVELY. Pay close attention, listen well. You should not fail to pay attention
to the Dharma which I speak. THINK UPON IT WELL, AND BE
MINDFUL OF IT; I WILL EXPLAIN IT IN DETAIL FOR YOUR SAKE.
I will now delineate the true, wonderful Dharma.

After Shakyamuni Buddha said this, what do you
think happened?

AS HE SAID THESE WORDS, FIVE THOUSAND BHIKSHUS,
BHIKSHUNIS, UPASAKAS, AND UPASIKAS IN THE ASSEMBLY
ROSE FROM THEIR SEATS, MADE OBEISANCE, AND LEFT. Although
they were very arrogant, they still bowed to the Buddha
before they left. WHAT WAS THE REASON? THE ROOTS OF THEIR
OFFENSES WERE DEEP AND GRAVE AND THEY WERE OF SUCH OVER-
WEENING PRIDE THAT THEY CLAIMED TO HAVE OBTAINED WHAT
THEY HAD NOT OBTAINED AND TO HAVE CERTIFIED TO THAT WHICH
THEY HAD NOT CERTIFIED.   They could not hear this wonderful Dharma. Such proud people had not attained the
wonderful Dharma or certified to the fruits of Arhatship.
Still, they claimed that they had done so. Although they
had not yet become Buddhas, they said that they had done
so. What they had not attained, they said that they had
attained. They claimed to have wisdom which they did not
have. They said that they themselves were not bad at all.
They said they were better than everyone else. These were
the   strange things they said. Consequently, they lost
their chance to hear *The Wonderful Dharma Lotus Flower Sutra.*

THE WORLD HONORED ONE REMAINED SILENT AND DID NOT
RESTRAIN THEM. He didn't tell them not to go; he didn't
stop them. THE BUDDHA THEN TOLD SHARIPUTRA, "MY ASSEMBLY
HAS NOW BEEN CLEARED OF ITS BRANCHES AND LEAVES AND ONLY
THE TRUNKS REMAIN." Here the analogy of the chaff and
the grain may be applied. The grain has been separated
from the chaff. The pure, real substance alone remains.
All the extraneous matter is gone. Those people with
offenses all have left; they are like the chaff, the
twigs, and the leaves. Those people who remain all have
blessings. They are the trunk, the basic, true substance.
They are the disciples who have faith. Those without
faith are like the twigs and branches; they are insincere.

For example, one disciple here took the precepts and
now has run off. He is like the five thousand who left.
He studied the Buddhadharma for several months and fig-
ured that he and his brother had both become enlightened.
He's just cheating the world.

"SHARIPUTRA, IT IS EXCELLENT THAT THOSE OF OVER-
WEENING PRIDE HAVE LEFT, because now they won't be able

to exert their bad influence on others. YOU SHOULD NOW
LISTEN WELL AND I SHALL SPEAK IT FOR YOU. Don't run off!
I am now going to speak the Dharma for those of you who
sincerely believe.
    SHARIPUTRA SAID, "SO BE IT, WORLD HONORED ONE. I
WISH JOYFULLY TO HEAR IT." We all wish happily and
joyfully to hear the Buddha speak the Dharma, the true,
real *Wonderful Dharma Lotus Flower Sutra.*

Sutra: (T.262,7a15)

61-64 The Buddha told Shariputra, "A wonderful Dharma such as this

is spoken only occasionally by the Buddhas, the Thus Come Ones,

just as the udumbara flower appears but once in a great while.

    65 "Shariputra, you should all believe that which the Buddha
                                                66-67
says, for his words are not vain or false. Shariputra all the

Buddhas speak the Dharma in accord with what is appropriate, but
                                            68
its purport is difficult to understand. What is the reason? I

extensively speak all dharmas by means of countless expedient

   devices, various causes and conditions, analogies, and expressions.
69
This Dharma cannot be understood through deliberation or discrim-
                                            70-71 72
ination. Only the Buddhas alone can know it. Why is this? All

the Buddhas, the World Honored Ones, appear in the world only

because of the causes and conditions of the one great matter."

Commentary:

    Shakyamuni Buddha had just informed Shariputra that
he was about to speak the Sutra. Why? Because he requested
it three times. It was clear that Shariputra was sincere,
and so the Buddha agreed to speak it.
    Now, THE BUDDHA TOLD SHARIPUTRA, "A WONDERFUL DHARMA
SUCH AS THIS IS SPOKEN ONLY OCCASIONALLY BY THE BUDDHAS,
THE THUS COME ONES. "Such as this" is a phrase which
points to the Dharma. The wonderful Dharma is "thus."
Were it not "thus" it would not be the wonderful Dharma.
So, the wonderful Dharma is just like that. It's just
the wonderful Dharma.
    It's just like what?
    Not like anything. Were it like something, it would
turn into something which is marked. Not like anything,
it is the unmarked Real Mark of all Dharmas. The unmarked
Real Mark is the genuine, real, wonderful Dharma.

The wonderful Dharma is only spoken rarely, when
the proper affinities have matured, JUST AS THE UDUMBARA
FLOWER APPEARS BUT ONCE IN A GREAT WHILE.   Udumbara
is a Sanskrit word which means "auspicious portent."[1]
This flower blooms but briefly once every three thousand
years; therefore, it is most valuable and rare. The wonderful Dharma is like this flower.

SHARIPUTRA, YOU SHOULD ALL BELIEVE THAT WHICH THE
BUDDHA SAYS, FOR HIS WORDS ARE NOT VAIN OR FALSE.   All
of you Sound Hearers, Conditioned Enlightened Ones and
others, ought to believe the speech of the Buddha. What
the Buddha says contains nothing false, nothing unreal.
It is all true and not false. Take care not to become
doubtful.

SHARIPUTRA, ALL THE BUDDHAS SPEAK THE DHARMA IN
ACCORD WITH WHAT IS APPROPRIATE.   Although it is wonderful Dharma which opens the provisional to reveal the
real, the Buddha manifests the provisional for the sake
of the real. For the sake of the true, real Dharma, he
employs clever expedient devices and speaks the Dharma
in accord with what is appropriate. He takes a look at
the potential and then dispenses the teaching, speaking
Dharma suited to the person being taught.

BUT ITS PURPORT IS DIFFICULT TO UNDERSTAND. In the
Dharma the Buddha speaks, one meaning is complete with
limitless meanings; one word is complete with the wonderful principles of limitless words. So, one meaning
encompasses limitless meanings, limitless meanings re-
vert back to one doctrine. Therefore, its purport is
difficult to understand. The doctrines are not easy to
assimilate.

WHAT IS THE REASON? Why can't they be readily understood? I EXTENSIVELY SPEAK ALL DHARMAS BY MEANS OF COUNT-
LESS EXPEDIENT DEVICES, VARIOUS CAUSES AND CONDITIONS,
ANALOGIES, AND EXPRESSIONS. From the time I realized
Buddhahood, I have used a countless number of Dharma-
doors of expedient devices, for the sake of the real
manifesting the provisional. I also use all kinds of
causes and conditions to teach living beings. I expound
upon all the Dharmas.

THIS DHARMA CANNOT BE UNDERSTOOD THROUGH DELIBERATION
OR DISCRIMINATION. Although various causes and conditions,
analogies and expressions are used to expound all the
dharmas, the Dharma itself is not easy to understand. You
can't use your conscious mind to understand it. You can't

---

[1] 瑞應華 -*jui ying hua.*

use your sixth (mind) consciousness, the discriminating consciousness, or the seventh consciousness, the deliberating consciousness, to try and figure out the doctrines of the Buddha.

ONLY THE BUDDHAS ALONE CAN KNOW IT. Only the Buddhas and the Buddha can know this dharma.

WHY IS THIS? What is the principle at work here?

ALL THE BUDDHAS, THE WORLD HONORED ONES, APPEAR IN THE WORLD ONLY BECAUSE OF THE CAUSES AND CONDITIONS OF THE ONE GREAT MATTER.

What are the causes and conditions of the one great matter? Each of us should think it over. What matter is our "great matter?" Shakyamuni Buddha manifested in the world for the sake of the causes and conditions of the one great matter. What great matter is it?

What is it? I will tell you: The great matter is not a small matter. Were it a small matter it wouldn't be called a great matter. Do you understand? That's a very simple explanation.

There is still another very profound explanation, but you will have to think it over and discover it for yourselves.

It's extremely wonderful. Wonderful to what level? Wonderful to the level that it can't be thought about. It's just inconceivable. Previously, it was already explained that it cannot be understood through deliberation or discrimination and so now in thinking about it we are completely wrong. We are discriminating and that is also a mistake. Not discriminating, not deliberating--that is just the wonderful Dharma. I asked you to answer the question, but the question does not need to be answered.

"Then why did you ask it?"

Why shouldn't I have asked it? If you can answer me as to why I shouldn't have asked it, then--I won't ask. Why is there no answer? Because Shakyamuni Buddha has now entered Nirvana, and really only Shakyamuni Buddha is qualified to judge an answer to that question. I'm not qualified to do so. So, the best thing to do would be to forget it. I believe that you all can't forget it. Why can't you forget this question? Because it deals with the causes and conditions of the GREAT matter. If it were the causes and conditions of some small matter, you'd be able to forget it. But how could you forget the causes and conditions of the GREAT matter? You can't forget it.

If you can't forget it, what's to be done? We should understand it. Although I talk about it back and forth I still haven't told you what the causes and conditions of the great matter are. I won't stall around and

keep you in suspense any longer. I'll--Here, it's like
...I hold up my closed fist and ask you: What do I have
in my hand? Take a look! What is it?

You don't know? That, too, is a cause and a condition of the one great matter. See? What's in it? I
open my hand--Nothing at all! The causes and conditions
of the one great matter are also just like that.

The causes and conditions of the great matter are
simply *no matter* at all. No matter, no affair, so Shakyamuni Buddha had to find something to occupy himself with.
It was just for the sake of speaking *The Dharma Flower
Sutra* that the Buddha mentions the causes and conditions
of the one great matter.

And what is said in *The Dharma Flower Sutra?* It speaks
of the wonderful Dharma. And what is the wonderful
Dharma? Do not think! Once you think, it's no longer
wonderful. In asking you about it, it becomes unwonderful. It can no longer be considered wonderful.

"Then what are we listening to the Sutras for," you
ask. "Wouldn't it be more wonderful not to listen to
them?"

Who told you to listen? You can not listen if you
don't want to. Go ahead. No one is forcing you to listen
to them. You may want to quit listening, but you can't.
You say, "I can too! I've thought of a plan. I'm going
to take some drugs and get so high that I don't know
anything at all. Then I won't be able to come and listen

Hmm...that's a wonderful Dharma too. But there is
another great matter which we should not forget. I just
told you to forget it, and you couldn't, but this is
something you should not forget. Since I have now encountered the causes and conditions of this one great
matter, I can't refrain from telling you. It is the
great matter of everyone's birth and death. Do you
understand it or not? The problem of birth and death:
Do you know how it was you were born?

You do not know.

Do you know how it is you will die?

You do not know.

Such intelligent people, and yet you do not understand the question of birth and death.

Yesterday some tourists came and asked a very
strange question. They said, "Why do you place oranges
in front of the Buddha?" A lot of you didn't hear it,
but since it was a potentially useful question I'm re-
peating it again today. Who did they ask? They asked
my tallest, and therefore highest, disciple. He stood
there, taller than everyone else, so they asked him.
But he messed up the answer; he wasn't clear. I was

rather irked and said, "How come you can't answer such
a simple question?" and I ran over to the Dharma-seat
and stood up on the platform, higher than my high
disciple. If I hadn't stood on the platform, I would
have been shorter than him. So I stood up and said
quite loudly, "You ask why we put oranges in front of
the Buddha? I will answer you. The Buddha likes to eat
oranges!!"

"Do you mean the Buddha can eat oranges?" they
said.

Of *course* he can eat oranges. We people like to eat
oranges, and the Buddha was a person who became a Buddha.
Therefore, I believe that he likes to eat oranges. Besides *I* like to eat oranges. I give the things I like to
eat as an offering to the Buddha. I give what I like to
others. I know that what I like to eat, the Buddha also
likes to eat. If I make offerings of oranges, he is
certainly not going to get upset.

That's the general gist of what I said, although
yesterday I didn't mention the "getting upset" part. I
said that he wouldn't be displeased. Anyway, when they
heard this it was a case of "seeing what they had never
seen and hearing what they had never heard." They had
nothing to say.

The causes and conditions of the great matter refers
to the great matter of birth and death. You should
resolve this matter of birth and death quite clearly.
Then you will have finished the great work.

There are the causes and conditions of the great
matter, then, and there also remain a lot of small
problems. If you want to understand the causes and conditions of the great matter, you must first understand
the causes and conditions of the small matters. If you
don't understand the causes and conditions of the small
matters you won't be able to understand the causes and
conditions of the great matter. Where do the causes and
conditions of the small matters come from? They arise
out of ignorance. Birth and death is the great matter.
Why is there birth and death? Because people are ignorant.

Once there is ignorance, then greed, hate, stupidity,
arrogance, pride and doubt all pop out! If there is no
ignorance, then all the little problems do not exist. If
there is ignorance, then there are problems, there are
birth and death. We should first become clear about
the causes and conditions of the small matters. If you
are clear about the small problems, you will be clear
about the great ones, just as small children grow up
to become adults. The adults get old and die. If you do
not understand the causes and conditions of the small

matters, you won't be able to resolve the great matter.
First of all, you must break through ignorance. When you
have broken through ignorance, the causes and conditions
of the great matter will automatically be ended.

Sutra: (T.262,7a22)

[73]"Shariputra, what is meant by 'All Buddhas, World Honored
Ones, appear in the world only because of the causes and conditions
of the one great matter?'[74-75] The Buddhas, the World Honored Ones,appear
in the world because they wish to lead living beings to open the
knowledge and vision of the Buddhas and gain purity. They appear
in the world because they wish to demonstrate to all living beings
the knowledge and vision of the Buddhas. They appear in the
world because they wish to lead living beings to awaken to the
knowledge and vision of the Buddhas. They appear in the world
because they wish to lead living beings to enter into the Path
of the knowledge and vision of the Buddhas."

Commentary:

Shakyamuni Buddha says, "SHARIPUTRA, I will tell
you something: WHAT IS MEANT BY 'ALL BUDDHAS, WORLD
HONORED ONES, APPEAR IN THE WORLD ONLY BECAUSE OF THE
CAUSES AND CONDITIONS OF THE ONE GREAT MATTER?" What
does this mean? I will tell you: All the Buddhas, the
World Honored Ones come into this Saha world because of
the great matter of the birth and death of all living
beings and because of the various types of karmic
retributions living beings must undergo. THE BUDDHAS,
THE WORLD HONORED ONES, APPEAR IN THE WORLD BECAUSE THEY
WISH TO LEAD LIVING BEINGS TO OPEN THE KNOWLEDGE AND
VISION OF THE BUDDHA. Their greatest wish is to lead
living beings to attain the knowledge and vision of the
Buddha. "Opening" the Buddha's knowledge and vision is
the opposite of "closing" the Buddha's knowledge and
vision. When was the door to the Buddha's knowledge and
vision shut? From the time of the first thought of ignorance. Ignorance shut the door to the Buddha's knowledge and vision; now, we are opening it again.
What is the Buddha's knowledge? The Buddha's knowledge is the heart of every living being. The heart is
complete with the Buddha's wisdom and knowledge.
What is the Buddha's vision? The Buddha's vision is

the Buddha-eye. If you open your Buddha-eye, you will clearly understand the Real Mark of all dharmas.

AND GAIN PURITY. Before we have opened our Buddha-eye, in all respects, we are impure and unclean. How are we unclean? Ignorance, affliction, coarse and subtle delusions, and various troubles cause our natures to become seemingly impure. It is as if we are impure, but basically we are pure. Because we have not opened the Buddha's knowledge and vision, we have not yet rediscovered our fundamental purity. Shakyamuni Buddha wished to lead all living beings to return to the root and go back to the source, to open the knowledge and vision of the Buddha. That is why he appeared in the world. He appeared in the world and manifested the eight signs of accomplishing the Way:

1. He descended from the Tushita palace.
2. He entered his mother's womb.
3. He dwelt in his mother's womb.
4. He was born from his mother's womb.
5. He left home.
6. He attained the Way.
7. He turned the Dharma Wheel.
8. He entered Nirvana.

THEY APPEAR IN THE WORLD BECAUSE THEY WISH TO DEMONSTRATE TO LIVING BEINGS THE KNOWLEDGE AND VISION OF THE BUDDHAS. The Buddha also wished to demonstrate the knowledge and vision of the Buddhas, to lead them to understand that the Buddha's knowledge and vision is inherently their own. It is not gained from the outside. This is precisely the point where Buddhism differs from other religions. All living beings can become Buddhas. It is totally egalitarian in that regard. Anyone who cultivates can become a Buddha. If you don't cultivate, of course you won't become a Buddha. It is not to say, "I am the one and only Buddha. You are not Buddhas." Nor is it to say, "You are a Buddha, and I am not." All living beings have the Buddha-nature and all can become Buddhas. Those of other religions maintain that there is only one God, the Almighty. Well, in that case, where did God come from?

"He was always there," they say. "You can't ask that. It's a sin to ask where God came from." How could such a question be a sin? Unless, of course, there was no God, in which case it would be a sin. If there was a God, it couldn't be a sin to ask. If you ask Him, he should clear the matter up for you. You can't say that if you don't understand something and ask a question about it that you are committing a sin. That doesn't make any sense at all. It's unreasonable. And after all,

God is just the ruler of the heaven of the thirty-three, Shakra.

Some religions say, "No, that's not our God. Our God is another one."

If that's the case, then where are you going to fit the lord of the heaven of the thirty-three? Unless you push him off the throne or persuade him to step down, he's still god. Actually, in Buddhism, god is a Dharma protector. But most people don't understand this doctrine They also don't understand the doctrine of no beginning and no end. They merely know that which has a beginning and has no end. As they understand it, everything began with God. Heaven and earth were created by God. God is eternal; he has no end. He lives forever and never dies. This is just what they think, however.

As to the Buddha: In the heavens and below, only the Buddha is honored. But everyone can become a Buddha. It is not that just Shakyamuni could become a Buddha and no one else is allowed to do so. The Buddhas of the ten directions have the same path. They are all the same. They do not say, "I am the only one. Nobody else can be like me." That's just being a dictator!

Now, the Buddha wants to demonstrate clearly that living beings are complete with the Buddha's knowledge and vision. It is not only the Buddha who has realized Buddhahood and who possesses the knowledge and vision of the Buddha. All living beings have the Buddha's knowledge and vision, but because they haven't understood the principle or obtained the strength, the Buddha wants to demonstrate the Buddha's knowledge and vision to them. That is why he has come into the Saha world.

THEY APPEAR IN THE WORLD BECAUSE THEY WISH TO LEAD LIVING BEINGS TO AWAKEN TO THE KNOWLEDGE AND VISION OF THE BUDDHAS. Once it has been demonstrated to you, you must awaken to it yourself. If you do not enlighten to it, but merely listen to others talk about it, it is of no use. The Buddha wants to cause all living beings to awaken to their inherent Buddha-knowledge and vision.

THEY APPEAR IN THE WORLD BECAUSE THEY WISH TO LEAD LIVING BEINGS TO ENTER INTO THE PATH OF THE KNOWLEDGE AND VISION OF THE BUDDHA'S. "Enter" means to certify to the attainment of the Buddha's state. Having had it demonstrated to them, having genuinely awakened to it, they must now enter into the path of the Buddha's knowledge and vision.

Opening, demonstrating, awakening and entering into the Buddha's knowledge and vision, living beings will be able to end birth and death. They will have completed the great matter and have nothing more to do.

That is why, after the Buddha spoke this doctrine, he entered Nirvana.

Sutra: *(T.262,7a27)*

"Shariputra, these are the causes and conditions of the one great matter for which all the Buddhas appear in the world."

[76] The Buddha told Shariputra, "All the Buddhas, the Thus Come Ones, teach and transform only Bodhisattvas.[77] All their actions are always for the one matter, and that is only to demonstrate and enlighten[3] living beings to the Buddha's knowledge and vision. Shariputra, in speaking Dharma to living beings, the Thus Come Ones use only the Buddha-Vehicle. There are no other vehicles, whether two or three.[79] Shariputra, the Dharma of all the Buddhas of the ten directions is thus.[80-81] Shariputra, the Buddhas of the past, by means of limitless, countless expedient devices, various causes and conditions, analogies and expressions, have proclaimed all the dharmas to living beings. These dharmas were all for the sake of the One Buddha Vehicle. All these living beings, hearing the Dharma from the Buddhas, ultimately attain the Wisdom of All Modes."

Commentary:

"SHARIPUTRA, the opening, demonstrating, awakening and entering into the knowledge and vision of the Buddhas which I previously mentioned, causes living beings to end birth and be released from death, to separate from suffering and attain bliss. THESE ARE THE CAUSES AND CONDITIONS OF THE ONE GREAT MATTER FOR WHICH ALL THE BUDDHAS APPEAR IN THE WORLD."

THE BUDDHA TOLD SHARIPUTRA, "ALL THE BUDDHAS, THE THUS COME ONES, TEACH AND TRANSFORM ONLY BODHISATTVAS. ALL THEIR ACTIONS ARE ALWAYS FOR THE ONE MATTER, AND THAT IS ONLY TO DEMONSTRATE AND ENLIGHTEN LIVING BEINGS TO THE BUDDHA'S KNOWLEDGE AND VISION. SHARIPUTRA, IN SPEAKING DHARMA TO LIVING BEINGS, THE THUS COME ONE USES ONLY THE BUDDHA VEHICLE. THERE ARE NO OTHER VEHICLES, WHETHER TWO OR THREE. Shariputra, you should understand that the Buddhas throughout the ten directions only use the Buddha-Vehicle. There are no Great and Small Vehicles. There are no other different little vehicles. "Two" refers to the great and small vehicles. "Three" refers

to the Sound Hearer Vehicle, the Conditioned Enlightened
Vehicle, and the Bodhisattva Vehicle. There aren't
three vehicles either. What is left? Only the One Buddha-
Vehicle. There is only One Vehicle.
    SHARIPUTRA, THE DHARMA OF ALL THE BUDDHAS OF THE TEN
DIRECTIONS IS THUS. They speak the Dharma in the same
way. They also say that there is only the One Buddha-
Vehicle, and there are no other vehicles.
    SHARIPUTRA, THE BUDDHAS OF THE PAST, BY MEANS OF
LIMITLESS, COUNTLESS EXPEDIENT DEVICES, VARIOUS CAUSES
AND CONDITIONS...all kinds of causes and conditions to
teach living beings. They say, "If you plant good causes
you will reap good fruit. If you plant evil causes you
will reap evil fruit. Goodness brings good rewards; evil
brings evil retribution. These various kinds of causes
and conditions concerning the operations of cause and
effect, along with ANALOGIES AND EXPRESSIONS, were used
to clarify the doctrine. The Buddhas HAVE PROCLAIMED ALL
THE DHARMAS TO LIVING BEINGS. THESE DHARMAS WERE ALL FOR
THE SAKE OF THE ONE BUDDHA-VEHICLE. Although he spoke
of the Great and Small Vehicles and of the Three Vehicles
the Buddha's ultimate wish, his primary intention, was
only to speak the Buddha-Vehicle and guide living beings
to the quick realization of the Buddha Path.
    ALL THESE LIVING BEINGS, HEARING THE DHARMA FROM
THE BUDDHAS, ULTIMATELY ATTAIN THE WISDOM OF ALL MODES.
There are three types of wisdom: First, there is All
Wisdom, which belongs to emptiness and which is the
principle of emptiness to which those of the Two
Vehicles certify. Secondly, there is the Wisdom in the
Path to which the Bodhisattvas of the Provisional
Vehicle certify. This type of wisdom belongs to existence
The existence meant here is a false, temporary existence,
not true existence. Those of the Two Vehicles certify to
the attainment of the "empty" while the Bodhisattvas of
the Provisional Vehicle certify to the attainment of the
"existent."
    Thirdly, there is the Wisdom of All Modes. This
type of wisdom belongs to the Middle Way. It leans
neither to the extreme of emptiness nor to the extreme
of existence. It is the wisdom of the Middle Way to
which the Buddhas certify.

Sutra: (T.262,7b7)

82"Shariputra, when the Buddhas of the future shall come into

the world, they will also by means of limitless, countless ex-

pedient devices, various causes and conditions, analogies and

expressions, proclaim all the dharmas to living beings. These
dharmas will all be for the sake of the One Buddha-Vehicle. Hearing the Dharma from the Buddhas, all these living beings will
ultimately attain to the Wisdom of all Modes.

83 "Shariputra, presently, all the Buddhas, World Honored Ones,
throughout the ten directions in limitless hundreds of thousands
of myriads of millions of Buddhalands, greatly benefit living
beings and bring them peace and happiness. These Buddhas also by
means of limitless, countless expedient devices, various causes
and conditions, analogies, and expressions, extensively proclaim
all the dharmas to living beings. These dharmas are all for the
sake of the One Buddha-Vehicle. All these living beings, hearing
the Dharma from the Buddhas, ultimately attain the Wisdom of
All Modes.

"Shariputra, all the Buddhas only teach and transform Bodhisattvas because they wish to demonstrate to living beings the
Buddha's knowledge and vision, because they wish to awaken
living beings to the Buddha's knowledge and vision, and because
they wish to lead living beings to enter the Buddha's knowledge
and vision."

Commentary:

SHARIPUTRA, the Buddhas of the past spoke the
Dharma in this way. What about the Buddhas of the future?
It's the same way. WHEN THE BUDDHAS OF THE FUTURE SHALL
COME INTO THE WORLD, THEY WILL ALSO BY MEANS OF LIMIT-
LESS, COUNTLESS EXPEDIENT DEVICES, VARIOUS CAUSES AND
CONDITIONS, ANALOGIES AND EXPRESSIONS, PROCLAIM THE
DHARMA TO LIVING BEINGS. They will expound upon all
manner of wonderful Dharmas for the sake of all living
being. THESE DHARMAS WILL ALL BE FOR THE SAKE OF THE
ONE BUDDHA-VEHICLE: there are no other vehicles. HEARING
THIS DHARMA FROM THE BUDDHAS, ALL OF THESE LIVING BEINGS
WILL ULTIMATELY ATTAIN THE WISDOM OF ALL MODES. The fin-
al aim, the end goal, is to cause all living beings to
gain the Wisdom of All Modes.

SHARIPUTRA, PRESENTLY, ALL THE BUDDHAS, WORLD
HONORED ONES, THROUGHOUT THE TEN DIRECTIONS, IN LIMIT-

LESS HUNDREDS OF THOUSANDS OF MYRIADS OF MILLIONS OF
BUDDHALANDS, GREATLY BENEFIT LIVING BEINGS AND BRING
THEM PEACE AND HAPPINESS. They wish to benefit and
profit all living beings and cause them to be serene and
blissful. THESE BUDDHAS ALSO BY MEANS OF LIMITLESS
COUNTLESS EXPEDIENT DEVICES, VARIOUS CAUSES AND CON-
DITIONS, ANALOGIES AND EXPRESSIONS, PROCLAIM ALL THE
DHARMAS TO LIVING BEINGS. THESE DHARMAS ARE ALL FOR
THE SAKE OF THE ONE BUDDHA-VEHICLE. Regardless of
whether they are of the past, present, or future, all
of the Buddhas in the ten directions speak the dharmas
only for the sake of the One Buddha-Vehicle. ALL THESE
LIVING BEINGS, HEARING THE DHARMA FROM THE BUDDHAS,
ULTIMATELY ATTAIN THE WISDOM OF ALL MODES. The ultimate
goal is to lead living beings to gain the Wisdom of All
Modes, to perfect Bodhi and to return to the state of
non-attainment.

    SHARIPUTRA, ALL THE BUDDHAS ONLY TEACH AND TRANSFORM
BODHISATTVAS BECAUSE THEY WISH TO DEMONSTRATE TO LIVING
BEINGS THE BUDDHA'S KNOWLEDGE AND VISION. The Buddhas of
the past, present, and future only wish to teach Bodhisattvas how to realize Buddhahood. BECAUSE THEY WISH
TO AWAKEN LIVING BEINGS TO THE BUDDHA'S KNOWLEDGE AND
VISION, AND BECAUSE THEY WISH TO LEAD LIVING BEINGS TO
ENTER THE BUDDHA'S KNOWLEDGE AND VISION. They want to
instruct all living beings in the knowledge and vision
of the Buddha, to cause them to awaken to that knowledge
and vision, and to cause them to enter into that knowledge and vision. Because of the causes and conditions
of the great matter, the Buddhas enter the world. The
Buddhas of the three periods of time, for the sake of
the One Buddha Vehicle, first spoke the clever, ingenious Dharma-doors of expedient means. Their final aim
was to cause all beings to attain the Buddha's knowledge and vision, the Buddha's wisdom, the position of
Buddhahood.

Sutra: (T.262,7b18)
84-85
    "Shariputra, I, now, too am also like this. Knowing that
living beings have various desires to which their hearts are deeply attached, according to their basic dispositions, and by means
of various causes and conditions, analogies, expressions, and
the power of expedient devices, I speak the Dharma to them."

Commentary:

SHARIPUTRA, I, Shakyamuni Buddha NOW, TOO, AM ALSO LIKE THIS. I now presently teach and transform beings in just the same way. I use various kinds of causes and conditions, analogies, and expressions to speak the Dharma to living beings. KNOWING THAT LIVING BEINGS HAVE VARIOUS DESIRES TO WHICH THEIR HEARTS ARE DEEPLY ATTACHED, ACCORDING TO THEIR BASIC DISPOSITIONS, AND BY MEANS OF VARIOUS CAUSES AND CONDITIONS, ANALOGIES, EXPRESSIONS, AND THE POWER OF EXPEDIENT DEVICES...Their thoughts of desire were not created through the habit patterns of one lifetime only. They have been created through patterns formed throughout limitless aeons, in successive lifetimes. For this reason they are deeply implanted in the field of the eighth consciousness of living beings. Because they are firmly imbedded there, they are attached to them and cannot set them aside. The power of such attachments is extremely strong; it is not easy to gain release from one's attachment. Knowing this, I follow along with the basic nature of each living being, with his habits, be they deep or shallow, and use the power of clever, expedient means. I SPEAK THE DHARMA TO THEM to set them free of their attachments.

Sutra:(T.262, 7b21)

86 "Shariputra, this is all done so that they may attain the One Buddha Vehicle and the Wisdom of All Modes.

87-88 "Shariputra, in the worlds of the ten directions, there are not even two vehicles, how much the less three.[89] Shariputra, all Buddhas appear in the world of the five evil turbidities, that is, the kalpa turbidity, the affliction turbidity, the living beings turbidity, the view turbidity, and the life turbidity.[90] So it is, Shariputra, that in the time of the confusion of the kalpa turbidity, living beings are heavy-laden with impurities; because they are stingy, greedy, envious, and jealous, they develop unwholesome roots. For this reason, all the Buddhas, by means of the power of expedient devices, within the One Buddha Vehicle, make discriminations and speak of three.

91-93 "Shariputra, if a disciple of mine calls himself an Arhat

or Pratyeka Buddha, but does not hear or know of the fact that all
the Buddhas, the Thus Come Ones, only teach and transform the
Bodhisattvas, he is not a disciple of the Buddha, nor is he an
Arhat, nor is he a Pratyeka Buddha."

Commentary:

"SHARIPUTRA," says Shakyamuni Buddha, "THIS IS ALL
DONE SO THAT THEY MAY ATTAIN THE ONE BUDDHA VEHICLE.
The Buddhas of the past, present, and future spoke the
Dharma for the same reason; it was all so that the One
Buddha Vehicle might be attained.
  "SHARIPUTRA, IN THE WORLDS OF THE TEN DIRECTIONS
THERE ARE NOT EVEN TWO VEHICLES, HOW MUCH THE LESS
THREE. Throughout the Buddha-worlds of the ten directions
there are not even Two Vehicles. You could say the Two
Vehicles were the Great and Small Vehicles. You could
also say that they were the two vehicles of the Storehouse Teaching and the Pervasive Teaching. How much the
less are there three? Three would refer to the addition
of the Separate Teaching. *The Avatamsaka Sutra* is the
Sudden Teaching, a Dharma for teaching Bodhisattvas; however, it also contains the "non-sudden" teachings. Thus,
the Avatamsaka Period was a Dharma for teaching Bodhisattvas. The Storehouse and Pervasive Teachings were
for the Arhats and Pratyeka Buddhas. The Separate Teaching was for those Sound Hearers and Pratyeka Buddhas who
were about to turn from the Small and go towards the
Great, to return to the Perfect Teaching. You could say
the three referred to the Sound Hearers, Pratyeka Buddhas
and the Bodhisattvas. You could also say it was the
Storehouse, Pervasive, and Separate Teachings because
The Dharma Flower Sutra is purely perfect and solitarily
wonderful.[1] "Purely perfect" means that it is only the
Perfect Teaching. "Solitarily wonderful" means that only
The Dharma Flower Sutra is completely wonderful. It is the
teaching doctrine which is purely perfect and solitarily
wonderful. The remaining teachings, the Storehouse, Per-
vasive, and Special, can't compare to it. Only the Buddha-
Vehicle is called the Perfect Teaching. The Sound Hear-
ers, Pratyeka Buddhas, and Bodhisattvas, those Three
Vehicles, are all provisional teachings.
  "SHARIPUTRA ALL BUDDHAS APPEAR IN THE WORLD OF THE
FIVE EVIL TURBIDITIES, THAT IS, THE KALPA TURBIDITY, THE
AFFLICTION TURBIDITY. THE LIVING BEINGS, THE VIEW TURBID-

---

[1] 純圓獨妙--*ch'un yüan tu miao.*

ITY, AND THE LIFE TURBIDITY. The Buddhas of the ten directions appear in the world to save all living beings.
They appear in the world which is evil and turbid in
five ways. There are five evil turbidities.

1. The kalpa turbidity. What is a kalpa? It's a
Sanskrit word interpreted as meaning "a division of
time." Basically, there is no such thing as time. The
past, present, and future exist only because living
beings discriminate. The kalpa is made turbid by the
evil offenses of living beings.

2. The affliction turbidity. This refers to the
five dull servants: greed, hatred, stupidity, pride, and
doubt. These five are the roots from which affliction is
born.

3. The living beings turbidity. Living beings have
all different kinds of good and evil causes and conditions as well as good and evil retributions. Everyone
has his own special evil karma. Living beings are also
turbid.

3. The view turbidity. The five sharp servants
belong here. They are: the view of a body, extreme views,
deviant views, the view of prohibitive morality, and the
view of grasping at views. They are also turbid.

5. The life turbidity. Living beings are allotted
a certain amount of time in any given retribution body.
This is called a lifespan. It is also turbid.

Our world is made impure by the turbidity of these
five, like clear water is made murky by a handful of
dirt.

"SO IT IS, SHARIPUTRA, THAT IN THE TIME OF THE CON-
FUSION OF THE KALPA TURBIDITY, LIVING BEINGS ARE HEAVY-
LADEN WITH IMPURITIES. The filth of their offenses is
extremely heavy. BECAUSE THEY ARE STINGY...miserly. This
means that they can't part with their money. They hold
on to a single penny so tightly it turns into water.
They can't even let go of a single cent. They are unable
to give. GREEDY: One who is stingy is unable to give,
but one who is greedy is not only unable to give, he
covets others' goods. Greed is insatiable. People who are
stingy and greedy will receive the retribution of being
extremely poor. Because they were stingy and never gave,
they have no blessings, no blessed retribution. Greedy
people not only refuse to give, but they are greedy for
other people's wealth. Such greedy hearts!

There's a little story which illustrates what can
happen to people who are just too greedy: Once there was
a very greedy person who died and went to King Yama. King
Yama asked him, "You are very intelligent. In your lifetime you never took any losses to speak of. Next life, as

a person, would you rather eat other people's food or
your own food?"

He thought it over. "If I eat my own food, that's
not as economical as eating other people's food and
saving mine." He said to King Yama, "I'd like to eat
other people's food. I don't want to eat my own food."

"Fine," said King Yama. "You can go be a pig. Pigs
eat nothing but things other people give them. They
don't have *any* food of their own." The person with the
greedy heart then realized that he was wrong to want to
eat other people's food, but it was too late. King Yama
would not alter his sentence, and the man had to go off
to be a pig and eat other people's food all day long.
That's what can happen when you're just too greedy!

ENVIOUS: Envy means that you are displeased if you
see anyone who surpasses you. You are JEALOUS of people
with talent. If someone is more gifted than you, you
can't stand it. This includes being covetous of other
people's goods or covetous of members of the opposite
sex. Jealous people eventually fall. If you are jealous
of others you may be reborn as an animal. Many of the
animals you see were once jealous people.

THEY DEVELOP UNWHOLESOME ROOTS. Because they were
greedy, stingy, and jealous, their accomplishments are
worthless. They do many bad things and consequently
they grow unwholesome roots, evil roots.

"FOR THIS REASON, ALL THE BUDDHAS, BY MEANS OF THE
POWER OF EXPEDIENT DEVICES, WITHIN THE ONE BUDDHA-VEHICLE,
MAKE DISCRIMINATIONS AND SPEAK OF THREE." Originally,
there is only the One Buddha Vehicle. There are no other
vehicles. However, if you started right out by telling
living beings to become Buddhas, none of them would believe you. That is why the Buddhas of the ten directions
and Shakyamuni Buddha all first speak of the dharmas of
the Small Vehicles to guide living beings from the small
towards the great. They speak of the Sound Hearer, the
Pratyeka Buddha, and the Bodhisattva Vehicles.

"SHARIPUTRA, IF A DISCIPLE OF MINE CALLS HIMSELF AN
ARHAT, says that he has already attained the fruit of
Arhatship OR A PRATYEKA BUDDHA, BUT DOES NOT HEAR OR
KNOW OF THE FACT THAT ALL THE BUDDHAS, THE THUS COME
ONES, ONLY TEACH AND TRANSFORM THE BODHISATTVAS, HE IS
NOT A DISCIPLE OF THE BUDDHA, NOR IS HE AN ARHAT, NOR IS
HE A PRATYEKA BUDDHA. Why isn't he? It's because, if he
had attained any of those positions, he would certainly
believe this wonderful Dharma which I speak. His basic
disposition would form a solid foundation for that faith.
If he doesn't believe, then he has not certified to the
fruit of Arhatship, Pratyeka Buddhahood, or Provisional

Vehicle Bodhisattvahood. He's nothing but a person of overweening pride.

Sutra: (T.262, 7b29)
94
"Furthermore, Shariputra, it should be known that those Bhikshus and Bhikshunis who claim to have attained Arhatship and to dwell in their final bodies before ultimate Nirvana, but who do not further resolve to seek anuttarasamyaksambodhi, are people of overweening pride. Why is this? It is impossible that any Bhikshu who had actually attained Arhatship should not believe this
95-96
Dharma, except in the case when the Buddha has passed into extinction and no Buddha is in existence. Why is this? After the Buddha has passed into extinction, those who accept, uphold, read, recite, and understand the meaning of Sutras such as this will be
97
hard to find. If they encounter other Buddhas, they will then obtain thorough understanding of this Dharma.

98 "Shariputra, all of you should, with one heart, believe, understand, accept and uphold the speech of the Buddha, for in the words of all the Buddhas there is nothing vain or false. There are no other vehicles; there is only the One Buddha Vehicle."

Commentary:

"FURTHERMORE, SHARIPUTRA," continued Shakyamuni Buddha, "IT SHOULD BE KNOWN THAT THOSE BHIKSHUS AND BHIKSHUNIS WHO SAY THAT THEY HAVE ALREADY ATTAINED ARHATSHIP, AND TO DWELL IN THEIR FINAL BODIES BEFORE ULTIMATE NIRVANA...They say that they are presently inhabiting their very last retribution bodies. After this, they will undergo no further becoming. They say that they have already attained the four virtues of Nirvana: permanence, bliss, purity, and true self. BUT WHO DO NOT FURTHER RESOLVE TO SEEK ANUTTARASAMYAKSAMBODHI. They don't push upward, vowing to seek the position of unsurpassed proper and equal enlightenment. They ARE ALL PEOPLE OF OVERWEENING PRIDE. They are all so intelligent that they have outsmarted themselves. They are proud, conceited, and self-satisfied; they've unmitigated arrogance, all of them.
"WHY IS THIS? What is the reason for this? IT IS

IMPOSSIBLE THAT ANY BHIKSHU WHO HAD ACTUALLY ATTAINED
ARHATSHIP SHOULD NOT BELIEVE IN THIS DHARMA. There is
simply no such thing as a Bhikshu who has already
attained to Arhatship but who does not believe in *The
Wonderful Dharma Lotus Flower Sutra.*

"EXCEPT IN THE CASE WHEN THE BUDDHA HAS PASSED INTO
EXTINCTION AND NO BUDDHA IS IN EXISTENCE. WHY IS THIS?
AFTER THE BUDDHA HAS PASSED INTO EXTINCTION, THOSE WHO
ACCEPT, UPHOLD, READ, RECITE, AND UNDERSTAND THE MEAN-
ING OF SUTRAS SUCH AS THIS WILL BE HARD TO FIND. Those
who can accept, uphold, read, and recite and understand
the doctrines of such Sutras as this will be rare indeed. It is by no means easy to find someone who can
explain *The Wonderful Dharma Lotus Flower Sutra.* Since no one
understands it, no one will be able to believe it.

"IF THEY ENCOUNTER OTHER BUDDHAS in other worlds,
THEY WILL THEN OBTAIN A THOROUGH UNDERSTANDING OF THIS
DHARMA, they will certainly comprehend this wonderful
Dharma, the doctrine which opens the provisional and
reveals the real.

"SHARIPUTRA, ALL OF YOU SHOULD, WITH ONE HEART,
BELIEVE, UNDERSTAND, ACCEPT, AND UPHOLD THE SPEECH OF
THE BUDDHA. All of you in the assembly, the Sound
Hearers and Bodhisattvas, should singlemindedly believe,
understand, accept, and maintain this Sutra and Dharma
spoken by the Buddha. FOR IN THE WORDS OF THE BUDDHAS
THERE IS NOTHING VAIN OR FALSE. THERE ARE NO OTHER
VEHICLES; THERE IS ONLY THE ONE BUDDHA-VEHICLE." It was
still to be feared that people wouldn't believe and so
he added, "Nothing the Buddha says is false; it is all
true. There aren't any other vehicles such as two
vehicles or three vehicles. There is only the one,
single Buddha-Vehicle. So you shouldn't have any doubts.

Sutra: (T.262,7c11)

99-100 At that time, the World Honored One, wishing to restate his

meaning, spoke verses, saying,

> Those Bhikshus and Bhikshunis,
>
> Who harbor overweening pride,
>
> The arrogant upasakas,
>
> Upasikas who don't believe,
>
> In the four-fold host, such ones as these,
>
> Numbering five thousand strong...

Commentary:

AT THAT TIME, THE WORLD HONORED ONE, WISHING TO
RESTATE HIS MEANING, to clarify it, SPOKE VERSES,SAYING,
THOSE BHIKSHUS AND BHIKSHUNIS/ men and women who had
left home WHO HARBOR OVERWEENING PRIDE/ They were
haughty and full of pride. When the Buddha was about
to speak the Sutra, they all left.
Why did they leave?
They left because they were too proud, too self-
satisfied. Now, think it over: Some people come here
and listen to one lecture and never return. Such people
have overweening pride. Or they may listen to Sutras
for a time and find it uninteresting and leave.
THE ARROGANT UPASAKAS/ laymen who are conceited
and proud. UPASIKAS WHO DON'T BELIEVE/ laywomen who
don't believe in this wonderful Dharma. IN THE FOUR-
FOLD HOST, SUCH ONES AS THESE/ NUMBERING FIVE THOUSAND
STRONG/ There were five thousand of them present at
the Dharma meeting.

Sutra: (T.363, 7c15)

Who do not see their own mistakes,

Deficient in morality,

And guarding imperfections,

Those of paltry wisdom have left;

The chaff within the multitude is gone,

Thanks to the Buddha's awesome virtue.

Commentary:

Five thousand of those present at the Dharma meeting got up and left. WHO DID NOT SEE THEIR OWN MISTAKES/
They did not see their own faults.DEFICIENT IN MORALITY/
AND GUARDING IMPERECTIONS/ THOSE OF PALTRY WISDOM HAVE
LEFT/ THE CHAFF WITHIN THE MULTITUDE IS GONE/ They were
like the chaff which blows away when the grain is
winnowed. They were so full of their own pride that
they did not know that they had faults themselves. They
saw the faults of others, not their own. They were like
the blackbird who criticizes a pig for being black. The
blackbird can see that the pig is black, but he doesn't
realize that he is black, too. People of great pride
will see the mistakes of others, but not their own. And
when it came to morality, they had outflows; they did

not hold the precepts perfectly.

Those who have taken the Bodhisattva precepts should keep them; those who have taken the Eight Precepts should keep them; those who have taken the Shramenera precepts should keep them. If you do not keep the precepts, then it is as if you had sprung a leak. You are like a bottle with a leak in the bottom, everything you pour in runs right out. If you keep the precepts, it is like filling that bottle with precious gems. You should always take care to keep the precepts, to accept and maintain them. Do not regard them lightly.

These proud people guarded their imperfections. They held their faults dear. The word for "fault" in the Chinese text 瑕 -hsia literally means "a flaw in a piece of jade." Perhaps one side of the jade is a bit darker than the other, or contains some other flaw. A piece of jade with a flaw is not worth very much. If we do a lot of incorrect things, it is as if we had such a flaw in our character. Breaking the precepts is like having a flaw in a piece of jade. Therefore, those who have taken the precepts must keep them

Those who left were like the chaff, the outside husk on a grain. They are also like the dregs, you might say, like the grains the distiller has left over when he makes wine. Those who walked out of the Dharma Flower Assembly were like chaff or dregs--not much use.

THANKS TO THE BUDDHA'S AWESOME VIRTUE/ They have already gone; they won't come and hear the Buddhadharma. Those whose good roots have ripened hear the Buddhadharma once and never want to leave. Those whose good roots have not ripened hear it once and then wander off for a while. Then they think, "I'm going to go listen some more." All those who come to hear the Buddhadharma have good roots, but some of them have good roots which have ripened, and others have good roots which have not yet ripened. There were five thousand of the latter kind in the Lotus Assembly.

Sutra: (T.262, 7c17)

These people, lacking blessings and virtue,

Are unworthy of receiving this Dharma.

The assembly is free of branches and leaves;

The trunks alone remain intact.

Shariputra, listen well:

101-104 The Dharma obtained by the Buddhas,

Is spoken for living beings
Through the power of limitless expedients.
The thoughts in living being's minds,
The various pathways they have walked,
The nature of their various desires,
Their karma, good or ill, from former lives,
The Buddha knows them all thoroughly.
Using conditions, analogies,
Expressions, and powerful expedients,
I cause them to rejoice.
I may speak the Sutras,
Gathas, or past events,
Of former lives, the unprecedented,
Causes and conditions,
Analogies or *geyas*,
Or the *upadesha* texts.
To dull-rooted ones who delight in lesser dharmas,
And who are greedily attached to birth and death,
Who, under limitless Buddhas,
Have not walked the deep and wondrous Path,
Oppressed by scores of sufferings,
For them I speak of Nirvana.
105- 106 I have established these expedients
To cause them to enter the Buddha's wisdom.
Never did I say, "All of you
Will realize the Buddha Way."
I did not say as much because
The time to speak had not yet come.
The time, now, is exactly right,
To speak the Great Vehicle.
The nine divisions of my Dharma,
Are spoken to accord with living beings;
Intending to lead them into the Great Vehicle,
I therefore speak this Sutra text.

107 For the Buddha's disciples, pure in heart,

Who are compliant and have keen faculties,

Who, under countless Buddhas,

Have walked the deep and wondrous Path,

I speak the Sutra of the Great Vehicle.

I predict that such people

In the future will realize the Buddha Way,

For with profound thoughts they recollect the Buddha,

Cultivate and uphold pure morality.

When they hear that they will become Buddhas

Great will their rejoicing be.

The Buddha knows their thoughts and conduct,

And speaks the Great Vehicle for them.

If Sound Hearers or Bodhisattvas,

Hear this Dharma that I speak,

Be it but a single verse,

They will become Buddhas, without a doubt.

Commentary:

THESE PEOPLE, LACKING BLESSINGS AND VIRTUE/ "These people" refers to the five thousand who walked out. They had no blessings and no virtuous conduct. In other words, they had no good roots.

ARE UNWORTHY OF RECEIVING THIS DHARMA/ They cannot accept the wonderful Dharma of the Great Vehicle because their good roots are not big enough.

THE ASSEMBLY IS FREE OF BRANCHES AND LEAVES/ Among those now left in the assembly, the Bodhisattvas and the Arhats, there are no twigs or leaves, no miscellaneous brush. THE TRUNKS ALONE REMAIN INTACT/ Only the trunks, the solid foundation, the Great Vehicle people with virtuous practice, remain. None of the Small Vehicle people are left. Only those with the disposition for Great Vehicle Bodhisattvahood remain.

SHARIPUTRA, LISTEN WELL/ listen attentively to what I am about to say. THE DHARMA OBTAINED BY THE BUDDHAS/ the unsurpassed, extremely profound, subtle and wonderful Dharma obtained by the Buddhas of the ten directions IS SPOKEN FOR LIVING BEINGS/ THROUGH THE POWER OF LIMITLESS EXPEDIENTS/ The power of limit-

less, boundless expedients leads living beings to
set aside the small and head towards the great, to
bring forth the Bodhi-heart and realize the position
of Buddhahood. I use expedient devices in teaching the
Three Vehicles. Originally, there are not Three Vehicles;
they are only provisional.

THE THOUGHTS IN LIVING BEING'S MINDS/ everything
they are thinking THE VARIOUS PATHWAYS THEY HAVE
WALKED/ all the different modes of practice they have
cultivated. THE NATURE OF THEIR VARIOUS DESIRES/ Each
living being has his own type of desires. Where do
these desires come from? THEIR KARMA, GOOD OR ILL, FROM
FORMER LIVES/ If they have good karma, the burden of
their desires will be a bit lighter. If most of their
karma is evil, they will bear a heavy burden of
desire. So, you can figure it out for yourself. Ask
yourself, "Are my thoughts of desire heavy or light?
If they are light, then my good roots arc deep and
thick. If they are heavy, that means my good roots
are weak and thin."

What is meant by "thoughts of desire?" Thoughts
of desire are just your afflictions. They are also just
your ignorance. They are the things you can't see
through, you can't break through. They are the things
you can't let go of.

THE BUDDHA KNOWS THEM ALL THOROUGHLY/ Using his
Buddha-eye to observe them, the Buddha understands
their dispositions completely. He knows all of the
desires and all of the thoughts in the minds of living
beings.

USING CONDITIONS, ANALOGIES/ various causes and
conditions and various analogies EXPRESSIONS, AND
POWERFUL EXPEDIENTS/ I CAUSE THEM TO REJOICE/ When
living beings hear the Buddhadharma, they are extremely
happy.

I MAY SPEAK THE SUTRAS/ "Sutra," a Sanskrit word,
means a "tallying text."[1] Above, it tallies with the
principles of all the Buddhas, and below it tallies
with the living beings to be taught. Above, it is one
with the Buddha nature. Below, it is one with the
causes and conditions of living beings to be taught.

GATHAS, OR PAST EVENTS/ "Gatha" is a Sanskrit
word. Gathas are verses used to repeat the principles

---

[1] refer to *DFS, Vol. I.* p.52.

set forth in the prose passages. Some of them arise
independently of the prose lives. An example would be
the verse in *The Vajra Sutra:*

"All conditioned dharmas
Are like dreams, illusions,bubbles, shadows,
Like dew drops or a lightning flash.
You should contemplate them thus."

Gathas often express key principles, such as these lines,
also from *The Vajra Sutra:*

"One who sees me in forms,
Or seeks me in sounds,
Practices a deviant way,
And will not see the Thus Come One."

OR PAST EVENTS: This refers to stories of the events
in the previous lives of disciples or Bodhisattvas.

OR OF FORMER LIVES: This refers to events of the
past lives of the Buddhas. THE UNPRECEDENTED: This
refers to stories of the events in the past lives of
the Buddhas.

CAUSES AND CONDITIONS/ ANALOGIES OR *GEYAS/ Geyas* are
verses which repeat the meanings given in the preceeding
prose sections, such as the verses being discussed right
now. OR THE *UPADESHA* TEXTS/ The Sanskrit word *upadesha*
means a commentary, a discussion of the meaning.

TO DULL-ROOTED ONES WHO DELIGHT IN LESSER DHARMAS/
The Small Vehicles people have dull roots. They prefer
lesser dharmas and do not like the Great Vehicle Dharma.
AND WHO ARE GREEDILY ATTACHED TO BIRTH AND DEATH/ They
are greedily attached to the revolving wheel of birth
and death; they don't want to part with birth and death.
WHO, UNDER LIMITLESS BUDDHAS/ In the presence of limitless Buddhas of the past HAVE NOT WALKED THE DEEP AND
WONDROUS PATH/ They did not cultivate the Way, the
Dharma which is extremely profound, subtle, and miraculous. OPPRESSED BY SCORES OF SUFFERINGS/ This refers to
the eight sufferings: Birth, old age, sickness, death,
being separated from what you love, meeting with what
you hate, not getting what you seek, and the raging
blaze of the five skandhas. There are also three sufferings: The suffering within suffering, the suffering of
decay, and the suffering of the life process. They are
tortured by the three sufferings, the eight sufferings,
and all the limitless sufferings. FOR THEM I SPEAK OF
NIRVANA/ The doctrine of permanence, bliss, true self
and purity.

I HAVE ESTABLISHED THESE EXPEDIENTS/ I have devised
expedient Dharma-doors TO CAUSE THEM TO ENTER THE BUDDHA'S
WISDOM/ to cause all those people who like the Small
Vehicle to obtain the Buddha's wisdom. NEVER DID I SAY,

"ALL OF YOU/ WILL REALIZE THE BUDDHA WAY/ I never said that the Small Vehicle people could also become Buddhas. Now, I am speaking the fine and subtle Great Vehicle Dharma. Everyone can become a Buddha. I DID NOT SAY AS MUCH BECAUSE/ THE TIME TO SPEAK HAD NOT YET COME/ When the Buddha speaks the Dharma, he first observes the causes and conditions to see whether or not the time is right. Right now, it is exactly the right time to speak *The Wonderful Dharma Lotus Flower Sutra*. THE TIME, NOW, IS EXACTLY RIGHT/ TO SPEAK THE GREAT VEHICLE/

THE NINE DIVISIONS OF MY DHARMA/ ARE SPOKEN TO ACCORD WITH LIVING BEINGS/ The nine divisions mentioned above are spoken in response to the needs of living beings. INTENDING TO LEAD THEM INTO THE GREAT VEHICLE/ I THEREFORE SPEAK THIS SUTRA TEXT/ I first spoke the dharmas of the lesser vehicles. My aim was to lead them into the Great Vehicle and that is why I am speaking this Sutra now.

FOR THE BUDDHA'S DISCIPLES, PURE IN HEART/ WHO ARE COMPLIANT AND HAVE KEEN FACULTIES/ They are gentle, mild, intelligent and wise. They have the seeds, the basic make-up, of the Great Vehicle. WHO, UNDER COUNT LESS BUDDHAS/ HAVE WALKED THE DEEP AND WONDROUS PATH/ Why are they compliant and intelligent? It's because in the past, in the presence of limitless Buddhas, they practiced the profound, subtle, and wonderful Dharma doors. I SPEAK THE SUTRA OF THE GREAT VEHICLE/ I speak *The Wonderful Dharma Lotus Flower Sutra*. I PREDICT THAT SUCH PEOPLE/ IN THE FUTURE WILL REALIZE THE BUDDHA WAY/ In a future life they will become Buddhas. FOR, WITH PROFOUND THOUGHTS, THEY RECOLLECT THE BUDDHA/ CULTIVATE, AND UP-HOLD PURE MORALITY/ With hearts of the Great Vehicle, they cultivate and maintain the Buddhadharma, and uphold pure morality. WHEN THEY HEAR THAT THEY SHALL BECOME BUDDHAS/ GREAT WILL THEIR REJOICING BE/ THE BUDDHA KNOWS THEIR THOUGHTS AND CONDUCT/ AND SPEAKS THE GREAT VEHICLE FOR THEM/ Knowing the thoughts in the minds and knowing the deeds that they do, the Buddha teaches them the Great Vehicle Dharma.

IF SOUND HEARERS OR BODHISATTVAS/ HEAR THIS DHARMA THAT I SPEAK/ BE IT BUT A SINGLE VERSE/ If they hear so much as a single verse THEY WILL BECOME BUDDHAS, WITH-OUT A DOUBT/ They can all realize Buddhahood. There is no doubt about it.

Sutra: (T.262,8a17)

108 In the Buddhalands of the ten directions,
There is only the Dharma of One Vehicle;
There are not two or three,
Except those spoken by the Buddhas as expedients,
And those are but false appellations
Used to induce living beings,
So that he may teach them the Buddha's wisdom.

109 The Buddhas appear in the world
Only for the sake of this One Real Matter;
The other two are not the truth;
To the end they would not use the small vehicle
To rescue living beings.
The Buddha himself dwells in the Great Vehicle,
And in accord with the dharmas he's gained,
Adorned with the power of samadhi and wisdom,
He uses these to save living beings.
Having certified to the supreme path, myself,
The Great Vehicle's dharma of equality,
Were I to teach by means of the small vehicle,
Even a single human being,
I would have fallen into stingy greed;
But such a thing could never be.

Commentary:

IN THE BUDDHALANDS OF THE TEN DIRECTIONS/ THERE IS
ONLY THE DHARMA OF ONE VEHICLE/ There is only one kind
of teaching dharma. And what is that? It is the Great
Vehicle. THERE ARE NOT TWO OR THREE/ The Two Vehicles
and the Three Vehicles do not exist. Only the Buddha
Vehicle is real. EXCEPT THOSE SPOKEN BY THE BUDDHAS AS
EXPEDIENTS/ However, although it is said that there is
only the Buddha Vehicle, and that the Two Vehicles and
Three Vehicles do not exist, still, because he wishes to
teach and transform living beings, the Buddha sets up
expedient Dharma-doors. He speaks of the Small Vehicle
and the Great Vehicle. He establishes the lesser

vehicle to lead living beings towards the Great Vehicle.
AND THOSE ARE BUT FALSE APPELLATIONS/ They are just
false names; they correspond to nothing in reality.
USED TO INDUCE LIVING BEINGS/ to teach and transform
living beings and cause them to cultivate the easy first
and then later to seek the Great Vehicle, the Buddha
Vehicle. SO THAT HE MAY TEACH THEM THE BUDDHA'S WISDOM/
Because he leads and guides living beings, they eventually
attain the Buddha's wisdom. ALL BUDDHAS APPEAR IN THE
WORLD/ ONLY FOR THE SAKE OF THIS ONE REAL MATTER/ It's
always for the same reason. THE OTHER TWO ARE NOT THE
TRUTH/ The Two Vehicles and the Three Vehicles are
not real. TO THE END THEY WOULD NOT USE THE SMALL
VEHICLE/ TO RESCUE LIVING BEINGS/ The Buddhas would
never, ever use the teaching doctrines of the Small
Vehicle to teach living beings.

THE BUDDHA HIMSELF DWELLS IN THE GREAT VEHICLE/
The Buddha himself abides in the Great Vehicle Dharma,
that is, in the Buddha Vehicle. AND IN ACCORD WITH
THE DHARMAS HE HAS GAINED/ The Dharma he attained in
the Bodhimanda is true, real, and is not a provisional
device. ADORNED WITH THE POWER OF SAMADHI AND WISDOM.
The Buddha has Ten Powers. Previously, when I lectured
the prose passage, I should have mentioned them, but I
deliberately did not so that those of you who like to
study the Buddhadharma could wait nervously for awhile
until the verse section to have them explained.

The Buddha has Ten Powers, ten kinds of wisdom
powers. They are:

1. The wisdom power of knowing points of enlightenment and non-enlightenment. That is, the Buddha is
aware, enlightened to the point of what is enlightenment and what is not.

2. The wisdom power of knowing the karmic retributions of the three periods of time. That is, he knows
the operations of karmic retributions as they work in
the past, present, and future.

3. The wisdom power of knowing all the Dhyanas,
liberations, and samadhis. That is, the Four Dhyanas
and the Eight Samadhis, the first, second, third and
fourth Dhyanas, plus the Station of Limitless Space,
the Station of Limitless Consciousness, the Station of
Nothing Whatsoever, and the Station of Neither Perception
Nor Non-Perception. That's the Eight Samadhis.

There are Eight Liberations: a) The liberation in
which inside there is the mark of form, and outwardly
form is contemplated. b) The liberation in which inwardly there is no mark of form, and outwardly form is
contemplated. c) The liberation of the pure liberation

body wherein pure liberation has been attained. d) The
liberation of the Station of Limitless Space. e) The
liberation of the Station of Limitless Consciousness.
f) The liberation of the station of Nothing Whatsoever.
g) The liberation of the station of Neither Perception
Nor Non-Perception. h) The liberation of the samadhi of
the extinction of the skandhas of reception and perception.

There also Eight Victorious Places. When one re-
nounces greed and desire one attains a place of victory.
They are: a) the victorious place in which inwardly there
is the mark of form while outwardly a small amount of
form is contemplated. b) the victorious place in which
inwardly there is the mark of form while outwardly a
large amount of form is contemplated. c) The victorious
place in which inwardly there is no mark of form while
outwardly a small amount of form is contemplated. d) The
victorious place in which inwardly there is no mark of
form while outwardly a large amount of form is contemplated. e) the victorious place of blue color. f) The
victorious place of yellow color. g) the victorious place
of red color. h) The victorious place of white color.

These are the Eight Victorious Places. This means
that in cultivating these eight kinds of dharmas you
can renounce, can turn your back on, thoughts of desire
and attain a victorious and liberated wisdom. In the
first of the Eight Victorious Places it is said that inwardly one has the mark of form and outwardly a small
amount of form is contemplated. At this stage one's
samadhi power is not yet complete, and it is to be feared
that if a large amount of form were contemplated, one's
samadhi power might become scattered. So, a small amount
of form is contemplated. For example, one single corpse
is contemplated, not a lot of them. You watch one corpse
go through its stages of decay--swelling, turning green,
and so forth. In the second of the Eight Victorious
Places, not one, but maybe a hundred, a thousand, or
ten thousand corpses are contemplated: Corpses, corpses,
everywhere. They all go through changes--swell, rot,
burst open, are eaten by worms, etc. Actually, there
are nine stages of a rotting corpse, known as the Nine
Mark Contemplation.

To the Eight Victorious Places you add Emptiness
and Consciousness to form the Ten All-Places. These
three dharmas--the Eight Liberations, the Eight Victorious
Places, and the Ten All-Places--should be known by all
cultivatiors of the Dhyana School. So the third of the
Buddha's Ten Wisdom Powers is the knowledge of the
Dhyanas, liberations, and samadhis.

To continue the list of the Buddha's Ten Powers:

4. The wisdom power of knowing the superiority or baseness of the roots of all living beings.

5. The wisdom power of knowing the various understandings.

6. The wisdom power of knowing the various realms.

7. The wisdom power of knowing where all paths lead.

8. The wisdom power of the knowledge of the unobstructed Heavenly Eye.

9. The wisdom power, without outflows, of knowing former lives.

10. The wisdom power of eternally severing all habitual energies.

The Buddha has these Ten Powers and so the Sutra text says, "Adorned with the power of samadhi and wisdom."

HE USES THESE TO SAVE LIVING BEINGS/ He uses his powers to teach and transform living beings.

HAVING CERTIFIED TO THE SUPREME PATH, MYSELF/ THE GREAT VEHICLES DHARMA OF EQUALITY/WERE I TO TEACH BY MEANS OF THE SMALL VEHICLE/ EVEN A SINGLE HUMAN BEING/ If I didn't teach and transform beings by means of the Great Vehicle, but instead used the doctrines of the lesser vehicles, crossing over even one living being, I'D HAVE FALLEN INTO STINGY GREED/ The Buddha speaks of himself, saying, "If I used the Small Vehicle to teach even one single person I would fall into a singy, greedy, miserly attitude; I'd be stingy with the Dharma, because I wouldn't be able to part with the Great Vehicle Dharma. BUT SUCH A THING COULD NEVER BE/' It would simply never happen.

By the way, I didn't use a book just now when I explained the Ten Powers and Eight Liberations, and I didn't prepare them ahead of time. I just remembered them.

Sutra: (T. 262,8c28)

10-111 Should people rely, in faith, upon the Buddha,

The Thus Come One will not deceive them;

He has no thoughts of envy or greed,

And he has cut off all the evil in the dharmas.

Therefore, throughout the ten directions,

The Buddha alone has nothing to fear.

My body adorned with marks,

I brilliantly illumine the world.

Revered by countless multitudes

I speak the Seal of the Real Mark.

112

Shariputra, you should know,

That in the past I took a vow,

Wishing to lead the multitudes,

To be identical with me.

That vow, made long ago,

Now has been perfectly fulfilled,

For I have transformed all beings,

Leading them into the Buddha Path."

Commentary:

SHOULD PEOPLE, IN FAITH, RELY UPON THE BUDDHA/ The Buddha spoke to Shariputra, saying, "If someone believes in the Buddhadharma and takes refuge in the Buddha Way, in the Triple Jewel THE THUS COME ONE WILL NOT DECEIVE THEM/ The World Honored One speaks the truth, speaks of what is real; he does not speak falsely and he would never cheat the people of the world HE HAS NO THOUGHTS OF ENVY OR GREED/ He would never have thoughts of covetousness or jealousy. AND HE HAS CUT OFF ALL THE EVIL IN THE DHARMAS/ All students of the Buddhadharma should genuinely understand cause and effect. You must put the principles of the Buddhadharma into practice. For example, everyone is basically greedy. Once you understand that greed is wrong, you should, bit by bit, get rid of it. Basically, we all have thoughts of hate-Once you have heard the Buddhadharma and know that hate is wrong, you should, bit by bit, reform your hateful mind.

The same is true for thoughts of stupidity and jealousy. If you have thoughts of jealousy, greed, hatred, and stupidity, these are what is called the evil within the dharmas. They are evil habits that should be cut off. The Buddha says that he has cut off all the evil within the dharmas, but actually the Buddha has already certified to the position of great and perfect enlightenment, so how could evil within the dharmas possibly remain? Why does he say this? Because he wants to instruct everyone else to sever the evil within the dharmas. For example, why are you so stupid? It is because, in

former lives, you were jealous of those who had wisdom.
When you saw that someone else was wise, you grew envious and so in your present life you are stupid. Why,
in your present life are you very intelligent? The same
principle applies in reverse. It is just because in
former lives you were not jealous of intelligent poeple,
you *liked* for other people to be intelligent, even to the
point that, as people studied the Buddhadharma, the
clearer they became about it, the more you rejoiced with
them and praised them for it.

If someone studies and learns quickly, you should
rejoice and praise that person; you shouldn't get
jealous. Don't be afraid that others will surpass you.
"When everyone is better than me, when everyone else
becomes a Buddha, then afterwards I can become a Buddha,
too!" That is the resolve of the Bodhisattva. Take a
look at Earth Store Bodhisattva. He vowed to cross over
all the hungry ghosts in hell and to take them all to
Buddhahood. Ghosts are the epitome of evil, but he
didn't dislike them; he resolved to save them.

Someone wanted to know if it would be possible to
make a vow to save all the beings on the five paths of
existence at the same time, on the same day, in the
same month, in the same year. The five paths are the
path of gods, the path of humans, the path of animals,
the path of the hells, the path of hungry ghosts, and
the path of animals. Could you vow to cause them all to
become Buddhas at the same time? This can't be done. Why
not? In order to become a Buddha it is absolutely necessary that one first be born in the human realm in
order to cultivate the Way. You couldn't keep a vow to
cause all the beings of the five paths to become Buddhas
at the same time. Earth Store Bodhisattva saves the most
evil beings. The Buddha has vowed to save all living
beings so that they will become Buddhas, and he would
certainly never be jealous and think, "Now I've become a
Buddha, and I don't like the idea of you becoming a
Buddha. Why not? If you become a Buddha, then nobody
will light incense to me! Now one will bow to me, see?
So, how about if just I alone become a Buddha and you
guys get lost, okay?" He's not jealous like that. He
wants everyone to become a Buddha and be just like him.
In fact, it would even be nice if everyone else became
a Buddha before he did.

So, as you listen to the Sutras, whatever you do,
don't be jealous. If you're jealous--I'm warning you in
advance--with jealous, greedy, hateful, and stupid
thoughts, in the future if you don't fall into the hells,
you'll turn into a hungry ghost, or else become an

animal. Would you say that was dangerous or not? If
you're not afraid of falling into the three evil paths,
then go right ahead and hold on to your greed, hatred,
and stupidity. Go head and keep them.

If you think you'd find the taste of the three evil
paths not easy to take, then you should get rid of your
greed, hatred, stupidity, jealousy and contrariness. Why?
Because these thoughts are the evil within the dharmas.
Within the Buddhadharma they are evil elements. If you
don't cut off the evil in the dharmas, you are going to
fall into the three evil paths. If you cut off the evil
in the dharmas, you'll be born in the three wholesome
paths. At the very least you'll be born in the heavens.
But those who study the Buddhadharma shouldn't seek to
be reborn in the heavens. If you do, you still can fall
into the lower realms.

THEREFORE, THROUGHOUT THE TEN DIRECTIONS/ THE
BUDDHA ALONE HAS NOTHING TO FEAR/ He's not afraid.
People say, "I'm really scared!" Some people are afraid
of the dark. During the day, they are afraid of thieves.

What can be done?

If there are a lot of people around at night they
get jealous. "I was doing quite well living here," they
think, "until all you people showed up to pester me."
During the day when there are many people around, they
find it too noisy.

What can be done?

When alone, they are afraid of the dark at night
and afraid of thieves by day. If there are other people
around, they can't get along with them. Perhaps at work
they feel that they carry more of the load and a lot of
vexation arises. Just *what* can be done?

This all comes as a result of having evil in the
dharmas. So you're afraid of this and afraid of that,
afraid of too many people, afraid of too few, afraid of
having people around, and afraid of being alone, afraid
at night, afraid during the day. If something happens,
it scares you; if nothing happens, it scares you even
more. You're afraid of the wolves ahead of you and
afraid of the tigers behind you. You feel like there are
wolves up ahead and tigers on your heels. See how you
are? You can't stand still, and you can't sit in one
place because you're so nervous and excited. At night
you have nothing but bad dreams. Why? I'll tell you:
Because you have evil within the dharmas.

Why is the Buddha fearless? In the worlds of the
ten directions, he fears nothing at all. He is not afraid
to speak the Dharma. He's not afraid to teach and transform living beings. He's not afraid that living beings

will be hard to subdue. He's not afraid of anything at all. He's utterly fearless. Therefore, he alone is without fear.

It is said, "if you are afraid, you won't attain your goal." Today, one of my disciples said something very interesting. He said that when he took his tests he just wrote right off the top of his head. He knew his professor's mind, what he liked. And what was that? Drunken talk! So he scribbled his test at random and it was exactly to his teacher's taste. He got a very high mark. Other people take tests on tiptoe, as it were, as if standing at the edge of a deep abyss or walking on thin ice. They are scared to death and wind up getting very low marks. There's a very logical principle behind all of this. It wasn't actually because he knew his professor's mind, but rather because he wasn't afraid. He also lectures fearlessly. Even when his teacher is standing right beside him, he dares to speak, and when his teacher leaves, he continues right one speaking. In general, he just keeps right on talking. He speaks not at all badly, too.

Others are not afraid either. When they hear their teacher say that they should lecture on the Sutras, they refuse to be afraid and go ahead. When they talk, however, it sounds like they were beating people to a pulp with a wooden club. It hurts a lot. They may not be afraid, but their listeners are! They talk everyone into being afraid to listen! This, too, is a problem. In everything you do, you should seek the Middle Way. The Middle Way means that you don't lean off to the left or to the right; you don't go too far, and you don't stop short. The Middle Way is without shape or form. It is the wonderful way. If you don't unite with the Middle Way, then it's the unwonderful way. The Buddha is not afraid, and he doesn't make others afraid either. His fearlessness doesn't mean that the Buddha is so fearless that when living beings see him they are afraid of him. No. When living beings see the Buddha, they are not afraid. The more they listen to the Buddha speak the Dharma, the more they like to listen. They more they like to listen, the more they want to listen. They listen to the Dharma for several decades without growing tired. The more they listen, the more they like it; the more they listen, the happier they get. That's the way the the Buddha speaks the Dharma.

"Well," you say, "then how was it that when *The Dharma Flower Sutra* was about to be lectured, five thousand people got up and walked out? If, as you say, the more they listened, the more they liked to listen, why did all those people leave?"

That's a good question. In fact, five thousand
people did walk out; they ran away and didn't stay to
listen.[1] Actually, it wasn't a case of their not wanting to listen, but rather that they did not have the
virtuous conduct to listen. They were driven out by their
karmic offenses. As soon as the Buddha announced his intention to speak the wonderful Dharma, their karmic obstacles showed up and they couldn't sit still. They left
on their own. It wasn't a matter of being afraid or not
being afraid to listen, of liking or not liking to listen. It was a question of their karmic offenses being
too heavy. They may have wished to listen to the Buddhadharma, but their karmic obstacles revealed themselves,
and they had to run away. They became possessed by
demons; the demon-power overtook them. If the ones with
offenses hadn't gone, they would have influenced the
ones without offenses so that they wouldn't have wanted
to listen either. Perhaps, right when the Buddha was
lecturing, they might have jumped up, or yelled wildly,
or gone insane. It was really better that they left.
That was the question involved. So don't ask questions
about things that pose no questions.

So, the Buddha is fearless.

MY BODY ADORNED WITH MARKS/ Shakyamuni Buddha says,
"Adorned with the marks of a hundred blessings," I
BRILLIANTLY ILLUMINE THE WORLD/ My light shines through-
out the world. REVERED BY COUNTLESS MULTITUDES/ I SPEAK
THE SEAL OF THE REAL MARK/ I speak the Real Mark Dharma-
door, the Dharma of real wisdom, *The Wonderful Dharma Lotus
Flower Sutra*. If you understand *The Wonderful Dharma Lotus
Flower Sutra,* you will understand the seal of the Real Mark.
If you don't understand it, you can't get "sealed."

SHARIPUTRA, YOU SHOULD KNOW/ THAT IN THE PAST I
TOOK A VOW/ WISHING TO LEAD THE MULTITUDES/ TO BE IDEN-
TICAL WITH ME/ I made a vow to cause all living beings
to be just like me, non-dual, and non-different from me.
and from all the Buddhas of the ten directions. So, whoever is more talented than I, whoever is more intelligent, whatever happens, I am never jealous of them.
If someone can do a good job of lecturing on the Sutras,
you shouldn't be jealous. You should rejoice and praise
them saying, "They lecture so well. I just love to
listen to them!" No matter whether they lecture well or
poorly, don't become annoyed with them or get upset. If

---

[1] refer to pp. 409-411.

you get upset with them, the Dharma won't get through to
you even if they lecture well. If you don't get upset,
no matter who speaks the Dharma, you'll recognize their
good qualities. If you listen carefully, you'll understand the doctrines and gain the benefits of listening
to the Dharma.

THAT VOW, MADE LONG AGO/ NOW HAS BEEN PERFECTLY
FULFILLED/ I have now accomplished Buddhahood; I have
fulfilled my vow. I have saved those living beings I
wanted to save. Some have certified to the fruit and
others have brought forth the Bodhisattva resolve. FOR
I HAVE TRANSFORMED ALL BEINGS/ LEADING THEM INTO THE
BUDDHA PATH/ I have now led all beings to enter into
the Path to Buddhahood.

Sutra: (T. 262,8b8)

3-114If, when I met with living beings,

I taught them just the Buddha Path,

Those lacking wisdom would be puzzled;

Confused, they would not accept the teaching.

Commentary:

If, WHEN I MET WITH LIVING BEINGS/ Previously, it
said, "...leading them into the Buddha Path." The Buddha
has led living beings to opening, demonstrating, awakening, and entering of the Buddha's knowledge and vision.
In these lines the Buddha is talking about himself. He
has rightly certified to the Eight Great Freedoms of the
Self:

1. One body can manifest limitless bodies. That is,
one Buddha can turn into countless numbers of Buddhas.

2. One body the size of a mote of dust can completely fill the great thousand world systems. Why? Because it is free!

3. The Buddha-body can lightly float to distant
places. For example, it can lightly float, just like a
balloon, right up into space. The balloon can fly a long
ways to distant places. The balloon, however, is just an
analogy. Actually, this is just the free and wonderful
functioning of the Buddha's spiritual penetrations which
enable him to rise lightly in the air and travel to very
distant regions.

4. He can manifest limitless kinds of living beings
which always dwell together in one land.

5. All the sense faculties may be used interchangebly.

I explained this when I lectured *The Shurangama Sutra*. The
eyes can eat and the ears can talk! The six sense organs-
eyes, ears, nose, tongue, body, and mind--all function
with the functions of the other five. Each organ can be
used in six ways. The eyes can see and hear; they can
also eat and taste. They all can be used interchangeably.
Would you say this was wonderful or not?

6. He obtains the suchness of all dharmas, without
the thought of dharmas. Dharmas are empty.

7. The meaning of one verse may be explained
throughout limitless aeons. The doctrines contained in
a single verse may be explained for limitless, boundless
great aeons, and still the meaning will not have been
spoken to the end.

8. The body pervades all places, like space. Al-
thought it fills all places, it is just like empty space.
When I explained *The Shurangama Sutra*, I said that the
Buddha was nowhere present and nowhere not present. If
you say that he is in a certain place, he's everywhere.
If you say he is not in a certain place, he's nowhere
at all.

We say that the Buddha is like empty space. What
does this mean? Take a look at empty space: It has no
shape or form. The Buddha's body fills all places in the
same way. We are all living in the substance of the
Buddha's spirit. The Buddha is like a big person who
fills up the space between heaven and earth. We live on
the Buddha's body the way small bugs live on ours.
Sometimes, when we don't bathe for long periods of time,
we might get lice. In northern China, they have tiny
lice and fleas. But the lice and fleas don't know what
the people they live on are like. They can't see the
people, even through they are living right on their
bodies. We dwell in the Buddha's Dharma-body in the same
way. We cannot see it. Why not? Because we are right
within it. In China, there is a saying,

> Why can't you see the face of Lu Mountain?
> It's just because you are standing
>   on Lu Mountain.

Lu Mountain In Chiang-hsi, is one of China's most
famous scenic spots. It has a lovely view, verdant
forests, and breathtaking waters. Why can't you see Lu
Mountain? Because you're standing right on it! If you
backed away from it, you'd be able to see it.

And why can't we see the Buddha's Dharma-body?
Because we are contained within it. Basically, there
isn't any place that is outside the Buddha's Dharma-
body. That is why there is no way we can get outside of
it.

Then how can we see the Buddha's Dharma-body? We must apply effort in cultivating the Way. When we accomplish Buddhahood and are one, non-dual, with the Buddha, we will know what the realm of the Buddha's Dharma-body is like.

The Buddha has attained the Eight Great Freedoms of the Self. He teaches and transforms living beings according to his intent, and, however he speaks the Dharma, he is correct.

I TAUGHT THEM JUST THE BUDDHA PATH/ So the Buddha uses the miraculous functioning of spiritual penetrations, the Eight Great Freedoms of the Self. THOSE LACKING WISDOM WOULD BE PUZZLED/ Although the Buddha is compassionate in teaching and transforming living beings, those without wisdom, the stupid people, cannot understand him. If he taught them the One Vehicle, they would surely misunderstand him. Stupid people, no matter what you tell them, always waver between doubt and belief. Why do they waver? CONFUSED/ THEY WOULD NOT ACCEPT THE TEACHING/ They are too deeply submerged in their confusion. When you speak the Buddhadharma to them they are not able to accept it.

Everyone can know the events of their past lives. You can know what you did in the past. How can you know? Take stock of yourself; take a look at yourself the way you are now. If you have a great deal of compassion, then in former lives you did not kill many living beings, you did not violate the precept against taking life. Having a compassionate heart just means that you do not have a temper. You look upon everyone as you would your own blood relatives. You cherish others as you cherish yourself. If you have that kind of compassion, it means that in former lives you did not kill. If you don't have compassionate concern for living beings, then in past lives you did kill. It's like taking a look at yourself in the mirror to see what you look like. If you are extremely hateful, then in past lives, you killed living beings. Those who like to kill have big tempers and a great deal of fire-energy. From these two indications, you can figure out your own set of causes and effects. You can know what you did in previous lives by looking at what you are doing right now. So, a few days ago some soliders came to visit and they asked, "Do you believe that people can become animals?"

I said, "If you act like an animal, you are an animal. If you act like a person, you are a person. You don't have to worry about what you will become in the future. If, in this present life, you do things that animals do, then you are an animal. If you do the deeds people do, then you are a person. If you do the deeds of a Bodhisattva, you are a Bodhisattva. If you observe the precepts of a Bodhisattva and practice the Bodhisattva Way, then you are a Bodhisattva, although you're just a junior Bodhisattva, one who has newly brought forth the Bodhisattva-resolve. If you do the acts of a Buddha, you are a Buddha. If you sneak around like a ghost, then you are a ghost. Just take a look at what you do. Everything is made from the mind alone--that's the principle at work here.

How is it that you are able to come here and listen to the Buddhadharma? It's because in former lives you believed in Buddhism and so now you like to hear the Sutras lectured. Those without good roots would hear the lectures and think, "What a lot of nonsense; how boring!" and run off. So you see, everyone can have the Penetration of the Knowledge of Past Lives.

Sutra: (T.262,8b10)

115 I know that these living beings
    Have never cultivated good roots.
    They are firmly attached to the five desires,
    And, out of stupidity and love, become afflicted.
    Because of all their desires,
    They fall into the three evil paths,
    They turn on the wheel in the six destinies,
    Suffering utter misery.
    They take a tiny form in the womb;
    Life after life, it continues to grow.
    With scanty virtue and few blessings,
    They are oppressed by scores of sufferings,
    They enter the dense forest of deviant views,
    Those of existence, non-existence, and the like.
    They become dependent on those views--
    Sixty-two of them in all.
    Deeply attached to illusory dharmas,
    They cling to them firmly and cannot let them go.
    Arrogant, they brag of their loftiness;

They are flatterers, their hearts insincere.

Throughout ten billion aeons,

They never hear the Buddha's name,

Nor do they hear the proper Dharma.

Such people are difficult to save.

Commentary:

    I KNOW THAT THESE LIVING BEINGS/ HAVE NEVER CULTI-
VATED GOOD ROOTS/ In former lives, they did not cultivate good roots, and so they are stupid. Those people
who have cultivated good roots are intelligent, not
stupid.
    "Do I have good roots or not?" you ask.
    Don't ask whether or not you have good roots. Ask
whether or not you choose to cultivate in accord with
the Dharma. If you rely upon the Buddhadharma to cultivate, practice and uphold it, and keep the precepts,
then even if you didn't have good roots, you would develop them. If you don't cultivate according to Dharma,
and, having taken the precepts, fail to observe them,
and you do no good deeds, then you would soon have no
good roots at all. There's a saying about selfishness:
            If I could benefit all under heaven
                by pulling a single hair out of my head,
            I wouldn't do it.
Selfish people wouldn't do a good deed the size of one
single hair to benefit someone else. If they could
benefit everyone in the whole world by pulling out just
one hair from their heads, they wouldn't do it. They
think, "Well, if I pulled out one of my hairs it would
hurt a lot and what difference does it make to me
whether or not everyone under heaven gain benefits
anyway? So what? What's in it for me? I'm not going to
do it." If you're like that, if you don't cultivate in
accord with the Dharma, then even if you had good roots,
you soon would have none. If you cultivate in accord
with Dharma, then even if you don't have good roots,
you'll get them. Don't ask whether or not you have good
roots.
    I'll tell you something even more profound: If you
didn't have good roots, there is absolutely no way that
you would be able to come and hear the Buddhadharma.
You wouldn't have the necessary causes and conditions
to study Buddhism. For example we who are listening to
the Buddhadharma now, especially to *The Wonderful Dharma*

Lotus Flower Sutra, in past lives have all planted good
roots. But you shouldn't ask.

I'm not going to answer your question, either. Why
not? If I said you had good roots you'd get arrogant and
say, "Look at me! The Dharma Master says I have good
roots, and no doubt my good roots are not small." You'd
get stuck-up. On the other hand, if I said you had no
good roots and that, in fact, in your last life you were
a pig or something and this life you're a person and
that is why you are so stupid, you'd think, "Oh, last
life I was a pig. Now I'm a person, but it doesn't mean
much. I think I'll do a few rotten things and go back to
being a pig." Such people always feel like there's
nothing going on. When they've eaten their fill, they
go to sleep. So I can't tell you whether or not you have
good roots.

Instead of asking me, as yourself whether or not
you can cultivate in accord with Dharma. If you can,
then even if you don't have good roots, you're getting
them. If you don't cultivate in accord with Dharma,
then, even if you have good roots, you're losing them.

The Buddha knew that these people had never in past
lives planted good roots.

THEY ARE FIRMLY ATTACHED TO THE FIVE DESIRES/ They
are stuck. They can't break through their desire for
forms, sound, smells, tastes, and tangible objects.
There is another list of the five desires: Wealth, form,
fame, food, and sleep. It is said:

> Wealth, form, fame, food, and sleep
> Are the five roots of the hells.

If you get attached to any one of the five desires, it
can drag you right down into hell. So we say that they
are the five roots of the hells. You could also call
them five chains. They are like heavy chains that drag
you into the hells.

Some people are greedy for wealth. They crave
material possessions to the point that they would do
anything at all, regardless or whether it was right or
not, to get what they want. Basically, one should not
covet wealth which is not rightfully gained. But such
people have no conscience in matters of material gain.

Form refers to beauty, especially the attractions
of the opposite sex. This is the easiest matter in
which people transgress. No matter who they are, when
men and women meet, their first thought is to determine whether the other person is beautiful or ugly.
Such questions are always foremost in people's minds.

If people aren't greedy for wealth or forms, they
may be greedy for fame and get locked in the chains of

of fame. They enjoy nothing but running around promoting themselves in all kinds of ways, advertising themselves. A certain layman had a card printed saying that he was president of such and such organization, head of such and such a group, and so on. The entire card was covered with his titles. What for? When you take a look at his card and see all his fancy titles, you're supposed to be very impressed. That's the way fame is, really important to people.

There are others who don't care for wealth, form, or fame, but guess what? They love to eat! They don't eat their own food either, but specialize in cheating other people out of meals. When they hear there's a party, they crash the gate, sit down, and eat their fill--a fish eye concealed among the pearls. Because of this, everyone looks down on them as gluttons and they are objects of scorn wherever they go.

Those who are not greedy for wealth, form, fame, or food, may be greedy for sleep. They can go without eating, but they wouldn't hear of missing their sleep. They sleep and sleep until their brains get all stuck together and they lose all their wisdom. They sleep themselves into stupidity. In Hong Kong and Taiwan people sometimes sleep to death! Why? Because they like to sleep. They sleep to death feeling extremely happy. They aren't aware of anything at all and die in their sleep, painlessly. That's the fifth root of the hells.

Therefore, once you understand the Buddhadharma, you should reform your bad habits. If you can't reform all five of them immediately, you can do it slowly.

AND, OUT OF STUPIDITY AND LOVE, BECOME AFFLICTED/ Because they cling to the five desires, they give rise to stupidity and grow attached to them. Because of their craving for the five desires, they think up all kinds of ways to obtain them. When their efforts are frustrated, they give rise to affliction. Why does affliction arise? Because they have no wisdom. They do not see their state clearly; they do not understand it. Basically, when one cannot obtain the five desires, one should reflect upon the principle and, returning the light, awaken to the futility of one's actions. Not only do they fail to wake up, they get afflicted.

BECAUSE OF ALL THEIR DESIRE/ THEY FALL INTO THE THREE EVIL PATHS/ Greed for food, greed for sleep, greed for fame, scheming for wealth, and lusting after forms-- all these various evil modes of behaviour generate afflictions. Because they are afflicted, they grow stupid. Because they are stupid, they fall into the three evil paths: the hells, the animal realm, and the

realm of hungry ghosts. They looked upon the five desires as too important. Unable to free themselves, they
let the chains of the five desires drag them into the
three evil paths.

THEY TURN ON THE WHEEL IN THE SIX DESTINIES/ Around
and around they go on the wheel in the six paths of rebirth. Suddenly they are in the heavens, suddenly they
are on the earth; suddenly they are cows, and suddenly
they turn into horses. Suddenly they are hungry ghosts,
and suddenly they become asuras. They revolve around
and around in the six paths because they planted the
causes to revolve on the wheel. SUFFERING UTTER MISERY/
Having planted the causes, they must suffer the retribution of turning on the wheel, all the misery and
wretchedness of the six paths of rebirth.

THEY TAKE A TINY FORM IN THE WOMB/ They may be
born from a womb. Perhaps they are born as a human
being or perhaps they are born as a cow, a horse, a
pig or--a mouse! See? Some people are afraid of mice.
If you are afraid of mice, then don't do bad things. If
you do bad things, yo may just end up in the ratpile
yourself as a friend of the mice. Look at mice: They're
dirty, filthy. You'd better be careful. Mice are also
born from wombs, you know. LIFE AFTER LIFE, IT CON-
TINUES TO GROW/ Taking a womb to be reborn--in one life
they take one kind of womb, and in the next life they
take another kind of womb. From small creatures, they
turn into large creatures. From large creatures they
turn into old creatures. In general, their karmic
obstacles continue to grow. The retribution of their
evil karma increases, life after life; it does not decrease. It just keeps getting bigger and bigger.
Finally, how large it gets, no one knows.

WITH SCANTY VIRTUE AND FEW BLESSINGS/ They have
very little virtue; therefore, their blessed retribution is also very small. THEY ARE OPPRESSED BY
SCORES OF SUFFERINGS/ They undergo all the different
kinds of suffering, the three sufferings, the eight
sufferings, the limitless sufferings. THEY ENTER INTO
THE DENSE FOREST OF DEVIANT VIEWS/ They run into the
thickets of deviant views. So many of them! How can
they ever find their way out again? THOSE OF EXISTENCE,
NON-EXISTENCE AND THE LIKE/ "Existence" refers to the
view of permanence and "non-existence" refers to the
view of annihilationism. The dense forest of deviant
views refers to the general list of sixty-two views.
THEY BECOME DEPENDENT ON THOSE VIEWS--/ They strike up
a friendship with all these views and come to depend

upon them. SIXTY-TWO OF THEM IN ALL/ There are a lot of
these views, but generally they can be listed under
sixty-two categories.

And what are the sixty-two views? I haven't explained them before, but now I will. You have all heard
of the five skandhas: form, feeling, thought, activity,
and consciousness. Those of outside religions think:
"Form is large and I am small. Form pervades the Dharma
Realm. I am very small and am within the form." This is
really stupid. How could they run inside of form? How
in the heck! It's ridiculous and it doesn't make sense.
But they make up this theory anyway and say, "Form is
great and I am small. I am within form." That's theory
number one.

Another outside religion comes up with the theory,
"Form is small and I am great. Form is within me." This
is the exact opposite of the first theory. Ultimately,
what form *is* they don't know, but form jumped right
into them! That's theory number two.

Another outside religion has this deviant view:
"Form *is just* me." That makes three. Another outside
religion says, "Form is apart from me." They have nothing to base their deviant views on. But that makes four
of them:

1. Form is great, I am small. I am within form.
2. Form is small, I am great. Form is within me.
3. Form is me.
4. Form is apart from me.

These four propositions apply to the remaining for
skandhas as well. For example:

1. Feeling is great, I am small. I am within
feeling.
2. Feeling is small, I am great. Feeling is
within me.
3. Feeling itself is me.
4. What is apart from feeling is me.

The same four propositions apply to thinking,
activity, and consciousness. The four propositions
applied to the five skandhas make a total of twenty
views.

These twenty views are of the present. The same
twenty may also be applied to the past and to the
future. Thus, the twenty views times the three periods
of time make a total of sixty views.

What about the remaining two views?

They are simply the view of permanence and the
view of annihilation, mentioned in the Sutra text as
the view of existence and the view of non-existence.

These sixty-two views make no sense at all, really.

Don't ask me how they arrived at them. They basically
have no principle behind them. They are just set up as
deviant views. If you look for some principle behind
them, you will fall into deviant views yourself. There's
no principle behind them, but we should know what they
are. We should also know that they are based on no
principle whatever.

DEEPLY ATTACHED TO ILLUSORY DHARMAS/ Those of outside ways are deeply, profoundly attached to these
illusory dharmas. And what are they? The sixty-two views.

THEY HOLD THEM TIGHTLY AND CANNOT LET THEM GO/ They
insist that their views have principle. "That's the way
it is," they say. "I am great and form is small," and
so on. They are stubbornly attached and refuse to change.
This is like certain people who are superstitiously
attached to their own religions. They don't seek out
true principle; they don't pay any attention to whether
it is right or wrong. They hold tightly to their be-
liefs with solid faith, faith even stronger than faith
in the Buddha or the Dharma Masters. If you tell him
to change he says, "No way! These dogmas were revealed
by our infallible patriarchs, and they can't be changed.
If you change them you've committed a mortal sin.   You
are damned to hell and lightning might even strike you
dead! I can't change the dogmas. I must believe in this
religion."

I have something to tell all of you: Whoever doesn't
believe in what I say may be reassured that you won't
be struck dead by lightning. If you don't believe in the
Buddha, you won't be struck by lightning either. Go
ahead and refuse to believe. Later, when you've thought
it over clearly, you'll come back and believe. Now, if
because you are confused, you believe in outside religions, that's all right, because when you finally wake
up, you'll come back to Buddhism. Why do I say this?
Because no matter what religion you believe in, it does
not surpass Buddhism. All religions are contained within
the Buddhadharma. However, there are long ways around,
and they are short cuts. If you believe in other religions, you'll have a longer walk. If you believe in
Buddhism, you've got a head start. If you believe in
Buddhism you'll understand sooner, get enlightened
faster, and become a Buddha first thing. So I have a lot
of disciples who listen to the Sutra for a while and
then run off. I don't pay any attention to them. If you
want to run, then run. When you've run enough, you'll
come back. Before you've run enough, of course you're
going to want to run. But it's no problem. It's just
like the five thousand who walked out. It's also like

eating. When people are full, they don't care to eat.
Once they get hungry, they start thinking about food
again. One's attitude toward the Buddhadharma works the
same way. If you think you don't need the Buddhadharma,
if you're not hungry for it, you may run off. When you
have run until you're hungry again, you'll come back
for some more.

Those of outside religions cling to their deviant
views and cannot let them go.

ARROGANT, THEY BRAG OF THEIR LOFTINESS/ They are
haughty and self-satisfied. They are always up on a
soapbox praising themselves. "Have you seen me? Me, me,
me--hah! You can't compare with me. Anything you can do
I can do better!" That's to hold oneself in high esteem,
to put oneself up on a pedestal. This is like a certain
person who came here and said that he was extremely high-
minded. This is just "bragging of one's own loftiness."
What is the point of doing that anyway? If your heart
is filled with pride, you are turning your back on the
Way. Students of the Way should be respectful of others.
At all times they should cultivate an attitude of
humility.

THEY ARE FLATTERERS, THEIR HEARTS INSINCERE/ What
is flattery? It's being a synchophant. When they see the
Governor coming, they open the car-door for him, pour
his tea, and light his cigarettes. They simply can't do
enough for him. They're not even that respectful towards
the Buddha! When they see a high official coming, they
invariably find a way to rub elbows with him. They are
not sincere, they are not straightforward. For example,
basically they may be out to borrow money from you because they know you've got it, but they don't come out
directly and say, "I'd like to borrow some money from
you." What do they say?

"Ah, today I need a little money. I think I'll go
ask so and so if I can borrow it from him." They say
this hoping that you will "volunteer" to help them out.
Their tactics are round-a-bout, crooked, and devious.

THROUGHOUT TEN BILLION AEONS/ THEY DO NOT HEAR THE
BUDDHA'S NAME. They don't hear the Buddha's name and
they don't have a chance to listen to the Sutras.

Those of you who are able to listen to the lectures
on the Sutras all have good roots. People without good
roots might come and sit for a minute, but they would
soon feel like they were sitting on needles. "Ouch!"
They'd hurry and get up and run away. Why? Because they
have no good roots, and they can't sit for even a second
before running off.

Here in San Francisco we lecture the Sutras every

evening. I ask you, are those who don't come here to listen to the Buddhadharma in the majority or are those who do come in the majority? This question is like the one the Buddha asked his disciples. He picked up a handful of earth and said, "Take a look. Is there more dirt in my hand or is there more on the ground?"

The disciples answered, saying, "Naturally there's more dirt on the ground and less in the Thus Come One's hand."

The Buddha said, "Those who obtain a human body are like the dirt in my hand; those who lose the body of a human being are like the dirt on the earth." Those who lose their human body and are unable to return in their next life as a person are as many as the vast amount of dirt on the Earth. Instead of being reborn in a human body, they fall instead into the three evil paths and become ghosts or animals.

Now, I can make an analogy, too: Those who come to listen to the Sutra lectures are like the dirt in my hand. Those who do not come to listen to the Sutras are like the dirt on the Earth. See how rare they are? Those who come to hear the Sutras are like gold. They all have good roots. Those who don't come are like dirt. You all have a very rare opportunity to listen to the Dharma. In all of America, you won't find another Buddha Hall where the Sutras are lectured every night. They may lecture once a week, but here we lecture every single night. This is really inconceivable. In the future you are all destined to become the pioneers of American Buddhism.

SUCH PEOPLE ARE DIFFICULT TO SAVE/ People like this, people without good roots, are especially hard to take across. In San Francisco, with its population of several hundreds of thousands of people, only these twenty or so are really determined to listen to the Sutras. Rare indeed! Those without good roots are hard to save. You can teach them the clear, correct, principles of the Buddhadharma. They will listen and know that you are correct, but they'll still oppose you. Would you say this was strange or not? Why does this happen? It happens because they have no good roots. If they had good roots, they would listen to the Buddhadharma and put it into practice.

In China, at Gold Mountain, there was one they called the "Living Buddha." He listened to the Sutras, and no matter which Dharma Master was lecturing, he would kneel and place his palms together, reverently listening to every word. Would you say he was sincere or not?

They called him the "Living Buddha" because one time he jumped off the top of the Gold Pagoda and when he hit bottom, nothing happened--he didn't die. He was able to cure people's illnesses, too. He used "Paramita Soup," as medicine. Paramita Soup was what he called the water he had just washed his feet in. He would add some fragrant ashes or some sawdust to it and give it to the sick person to drink. Once the sick person drank it, he would be cured.

In the West it is extremely rare to be able to attend a Dharma Assembly such as this one. Today, I spoke with my disciples about how important it is to lecture on the Sutras. In the future, in the Dharma-ending age, the Buddhist Sutras will disappear. The paper will remain, but the words will just fade away, and you won't be able to read them. The first Sutra to disappear will be *The Shurangama Sutra*. That is why, in coming to the West to spread the Dharma, I first lectured *The Shurangama Sutra*, the Sutra for developing wisdom. If you look into the doctrines discussed in the Sutra you will find that they are truly much more wonderful than any theories propounded by modern day science or philosophy, as the doctrines in the Sutra are ultimate.

Now that I have finished lecturing *The Shurangama Sutra*, I am lecturing *The Dharma Flower Sutra*. When I have finished lecturing it, I intend to lecture *The Avatamsaka Sutra* for you. That's even more wonderful! *The Dharma Flower Sutra* is called the king of Sutras, but *The Avatamsaka Sutra* is really the king of the kings of Sutras. The *Avatamsaka* is like a Gold Wheel-Turning Sage King, and the *Dharma Flower* is like a Silver Wheel-Turning Sage King. The *Shurangama* is like a Copper Wheel-Turning Sage King. They are the three kings among the Sutras.

Where did *The Avatamsaka Sutra* come from? After the Buddha realized Buddhahood, the first thing he did was speak this Sutra. When he spoke it, those of the Two Vehicles could not hear him. They couldn't even see him. It is said,

> They had eyes, but couldn't see the Buddha.
> They had ears, but couldn't hear
> the perfect, sudden teaching.

The Buddha manifested a ten thousand foot high body to speak the Sutra, and although they had eyes, they couldn't see it. They had ears, but they couldn't hear the perfect, sudden teaching. Those of the Two Vehicles couldn't understand it, and only the Great Vehicle Bodhisattvas were clear about it. Later, it was taken by the Dragon King to the Dragon Palace and it disappeared from the human realm. Later, the Fourteenth Patriarch,

Nagarjuna, "Dragon Tree," Bodhisattva, who had mastered
all worldly literature, used his spiritual penetrations
to go down to the Dragon Palace to take a look at their
Tripitaka. There he found the three volume set of *The
Great Avatamsaka Sutra*. The first volume contained chapters
in number equal to dust motes in ten great trichiliocosms.
The second volume had twelve hundred chapters and four
hundred and ninety-eight thousand eight hundred verses.
The third volume contained forty-eight chapters and one
hundred thousand verses. The standard Chinese edition,
translated during the T'ang Dynasty by Tripitaka Master
Shiksananda, contains thirty-nine chapters.

Since he had no way to remember all of it, he only
memorized the last volume. When he came back, he wrote
it out. He read it once and remembered it perfectly.
His memory was extremely good. That is where *The Avatamsaka Sutra* came from.

So, when we have finished *The Dharma Flower Sutra,* we
shall hear *The Great Avatamsaka Sutra.* Having heard the
three kings of Sutras and understood them, you will
then be able to understand all the other Sutras on your
own, without having them explained to you. Here in the
West, the Buddhadharma has just begun to flourish. It
is fitting that the Great Vehicle Dharma be propagated
in order to teach and transform the Great Vehicle Bodhisattvas. Don't see yourselves as insignificant. You are
all ones who in the past made vows agreeing to come
to America with me to help me propagate the Buddhadharma.
That's why I have now met with you extremely intelligent
Westerners who come here every day to study the Buddhadharma; this is because of a far-reaching affinity, a
cause which goes way back, and which was planted long,
long ago. I'm telling you the truth; you should not
disbelieve it.

Sutra: (T.262, 8b22)
116
    Therefore, Shariputra,

    I set forth expedients for them,

    Speak of the way to suffering's end,

    And demonstrate Nirvana.

    Although I speak of Nirvana,
117 It is not true extinction.

    All dharmas from their origin,

    Are ever marked by still extinction.

When the Buddha's disciples have walked the Path,

In a future age they will become Buddhas.

118 I possess the power of expedients,

And demonstrate the Dharma of Three Vehicles.

All the World Honored Ones,

Speak the Dharma of One Vehicle.

Now all of you assembled here,

Should cast your doubts aside.

The speech of all Buddhas is the same:

There is only One Vehicle, not two.

Commentary:

THEREFORE, SHARIPUTRA/ I Shakyamuni Buddha, say
that people are all difficult to save. Why are they
difficult to save? Simply because they are too stupid.
They are so stupid that if you teach them the genuine
Dharma, they don't understand it. They doubt it and
wonder, "That's why you say, but I don't know if it's
true or not. I don't know if that is the true Dharma."
I SET FORTH EXPEDIENTS FOR THEM/ I set up some provisional, expedient Dharma-doors, and SPEAK OF THE WAY
TO SUFFERING'S END/ I speak the Three Storehouse
Teaching so they may leave suffering. So it is said,

Know suffering,

Cut off origination,

Long for extinction, and

Cultivate the Way.

Everyone should know that everything in this world
is suffering. Knowing suffering, you should end suffering. That is why I speak this Dharma-door of ending
suffering. I speak the Dharma of the Four Holy Truths.
AND DEMONSTRATE NIRVANA/ "Demonstrate" means that I instruct the Small Vehicle people in the method used to
certify to the wonderful fruit of Nirvana: permanence,
bliss, true self, and purity. ALTHOUGH I SPEAK OF
NIRVANA/ I teach the wonderful Dharma of non-production
and non-extinction. IT IS NOT TRUE EXTINCTION/ However,
that dharma which I speak for those of the Two Vehicles
is not the genuine, ultimate Dharma of still extinction.
ALL DHARMAS FROM THEIR ORIGIN/ Why do I say that it is
not the ultimate Dharma of still extinction? Because all
dharmas basically, from where they begin, from their
origin ARE EVER MARKED BY STILL EXTINCTION/ The basic

substance of the Dharma is still and extinct. It is
"thus, thus."
      WHEN THE BUDDHA'S DISCIPLES HAVE WALKED THE PATH/
I have spoken the Small Vehicle dharma for these people
to cultivate. However, after they have cultivated the
Small Vehicle dharmas to perfection, they must still
return from the Small and go towards the Great, and
walk the Bodhisattva Way in order to be genuine
disciples of the Buddha. When they have cultivated the
Bodhisattva Way to perfection, then IN A FUTURE AGE THEY
WILL BECOME BUDDHAS/ In a future life they will certify
to the Buddha-fruit. If, in the very beginning, you
tried to teach them to cultivate for the Buddha-fruit,
to practice the Six Perfections and the Ten Thousand
Conducts, they would be frightened. They would think
such cultivation was to difficult. I POSSESS THE POWER
OF EXPEDIENTS/ I set up provisional devices. After I
spoke *The Great Avatamsaka Sutra,* seeing that those of the
Two Vehicles could not understand it, I set up expedient devices. AND DEMONSTRATE THE DHARMA OF THREE
VEHICLES/ I demonstrate the Dharma-doors of the Vehicle
of the Sound Hearers, the Vehicle of the Conditioned-
Enlightened Ones, and the Vehicle of the Bodhisattvas.
      ALL THE WORLD HONORED ONES/ Although I teach the
Three Vehicles, my ultimate aim, my final goal, is
still to cause all living beings to become Buddhas.
Not only do I speak the highest Buddha Vehicle, but
all of the World Honored Ones throughout all the worlds
in the ten directions, all the Buddhas, SPEAK THE
PATH OF ONE VEHICLE/ They return the three to the
one and open the provisional to reveal the real. They
set aside the teaching of the Three Vehicles to reveal the One Vehicle, the real teaching.
      NOW ALL OF YOU ASSEMBLED HERE/ Bodhisattvas,
Arhats, Bhikshus, Bhikshunis, Upasakas, Upasikas, ghosts
and spirits, all of the gods and dragons and the rest
of the eight-fold division, SHOULD CAST YOUR DOUBTS
ASIDE/ Get rid of your doubts; you should not harbor
doubts concerning *The Wonderful Dharma Lotus Flower Sutra.*
Don't be like a fox, who has doubts about everything.
When foxes cross the river when it has frozen over, they
take a step and then cock their ears, listening to hear
if the ice creaks. Will it hold them, or will it crack
and dump them into the river? They take a step, listen,
take another step, and listen some more. Although they
don't hear a sound, they still don't believe. With each
step they have to listen again. Foxes are full of
doubt. Those who believe in the Buddha, but who do not
have good roots, will half believe and half disbelieve.

Their faith is not real because they have not cast their doubts aside. Now, all present in the assembly are exhorted to cast their doubts aside.

To put it another way, why is it that some people half believe in the Buddhadharma and half disbelieve? It's because they are stupid. If they had Prajna wisdom, they couldn't possibly have doubts. But, because they lack Prajna wisdom, if you speak the true Dharma for them they hear it as false dharma. If you speak the subtle Dharma for them, they hear it as coarse dharma. They do not have the selective Dharma Eye. That is why they give rise to doubts.

THE SPEECH OF ALL BUDDHAS IS THE SAME: THERE IS ONLY ONE VEHICLE, NOT TWO/ The Buddhas of the ten directions say the same things. Why is that? They speak only the One Vehicle, the Buddha Way, the One Buddha Vehicle, the true real wisdom. There are not two vehicles. There's no Sound Hearer Vehicle, no Conditioned Enlightened Vehicle, and no Bodhisattva Vehicle. The Buddhas speak only the One Buddha Vehicle. They speak the Dharma-door of the Real Teaching; they don't speak the provisional teaching. This is called "opening the provisional to reveal the Real." They put the provisonal, clever expedient device Dharma-doors off to one side and speak only the wonderful doctrine of the Real Mark. So now, the Sound Hearers and the Conditioned Enlightened Ones should return from the small and go towards the Great, cultivate and practice real wisdom. If they don't put down the provisional wisdom, they won't be able to understand real wisdom. There is only one, not two, vehicles. There is only the Buddha Vehicle.

Sutra: (T.262, 8c2)

119-120

Throughout countless aeons in the past,

Innumerable extinct Buddhas,

Hundreds of thousands of myriads of millions of them,

A number beyond all calculation,

World Honored Ones such as these,

Used various conditions, analogies,

And the power of countless expedients,

To proclaim the marks of all dharmas.

All of those World Honored Ones,

Spoke the Dharma of One Vehicle,

Transforming beings without limit,

Leading them to the Buddha Path.

Commentary:

THROUGHOUT COUNTLESS AEONS IN THE PAST/ Limitless aeons on the past, a countless number of them, and these aeons were not small aeons; they were great aeons.

What is a great aeon? Basically, there's no fixed way to measure time, as it is not real. But, because living beings make discriminations with their minds, the past, present, and future come into being. Time in itself basically is without a past, present, or future. These three come into being through the discriminations made in the minds of living beings. In *The Vajra Sutra*, the Buddha says very plainly that there is no such thing as time. He says, "Past thought cannot be got at; present thought cannot be got at; future thought cannot be got at."

What is meant by, "Past thought canot be got at?" It's because what's past is past. If you say, "This is past," it has already gone by. You can't get at it.

As to present thought, if you say, "This is present," just as you say it, it goes by. The present does not stay. The past has already gone by and the present goes right one by, too. It does not stay in one place.

The future cannot be got at because it has not yet come. So why are you going out to welcome it? If it hasn't arrived, you needn't go out to meet it. The future just hasn't got here yet. The present can't be held in one place; therefore, it also does not exist. The past has gone; you shouldn't go chasing after it. The three phases of thought ultimately cannot be got at.

Speaking of the three phases of thought as unobtainable, in Szechwan there was a Dharma Master by the name of Chou who specialized in explaining *The Vajra Sutra*. Not only did he excel at explaining it orally, but he also wrote a commentary on it. He title his commentary: *The Green Dragon Commentary and Notes*. He heard that in the south, in Yang-chou, those who had left the home-life were investigating Ch'an and sitting in meditation and no one lectured on the Sutras or spoke the Dharma. He sighed and said, "These people are all the sons and grandsons of demons. In Buddhism, one should lecture on the Sutras and the Dharma. What's the use of sitting in meditation all day long?" So he put

his *Green Dragon Commentary and Notes* in two baskets,
fastened them to a pole, shouldered the pole, and
set out on foot for Yang-chou. He planned to lecture
on the Sutras there and teach and transform living
beings.

Just as he was nearing Yang-chou he saw a pastry
shop. An old woman was running the store. At that very
moment he felt a pang of hunger and decided to buy a
piece of pastry. He put down his pole and said, "I
would like a pastry please."

The old woman asked him, "Where are you from?"

"I've come from Szechwan," he replied.

"What are you carrying that load of paper for?"
ask asked. "Where do you plan on selling it?"

The Dharma Master said, "Ah! This is my commentary
on *The Vajra Sutra*. It's certinaly not for sale!"

"Really?" A commentary on *The Vajra Sutra?*" she said.
"In *The Vajra Sutra* there are three sentences I would like
you to explain for me."

Hearing this, Vajra Chou said, "For heaven's sake,
I wrote a commentary on the entire Sutra. I should hope
I could answer your question. Ask away!"

She said, "Dharma Master, as you comment on the
passage of the Sutra which says, 'Past thought cannot
be got at; present thought cannot be got at; future
thought cannot be got at,' I would ask you today,
which pastry would you like to take?"

With that one question, Vajra Chou's mouth fell
shut and he was speechless. He ultimately didn't know
which cake to take, that is, how to answer her. He
realized that his theories didn't hold water. Consequently, he put his commentary in storage and headed
for Kao Min Monastery to do some work in the meditation
hall. Eventually he became enlightened and then knew
that the entire Dharma storehouse can be understood
only through concentrated effort on real practice. If
you don't work hard, and only talk, you can talk coming
and going, vertically and horizontally, and your words
are nothing but the skin. You have not realized the
genuine principles contained within the Sutras. In
the Great Master Yung Chia's *Song of Certifying to the Way*,
he says,

> "With penetration of the sect,
> And penetration of speech,
> Samadhi and wisdom are perfect and clear,
> And there is no attachment to emptiness.

"Penetration of the sect" means not only can he
lecture on the Sutras and speak the Dharma, but he is
also able to investigate Dhyana and sit in meditation.

"Penetration of speech" means that he can lecture on the
Sutras and speak the Dharma. This is called "Penetration
of both the sect and the speaking." The "sect" refers to
the Ch'an (Dhyana) School. He understands them both
and therefore, "Samadhi and wisdom are perfect and
clear," Why has he penetrated the sect? It's because
he has samadhi power and wisdom power. Samadhi power and
wisdom power perfectly interpenetrate. Samadhi aids the
wisdom, and wisdom aids the samadhi. To have samadhi
but no wisdom is merely to peneteate the sect, and not
to penetrate the teachings. To have wisdom but no
samadhi is only to penetrate the teachings and not
to penetrate the sect.

The verse says, "Samadhi and wisdom are perfect and
clear/ And there is no attachment to emptiness." He
doesn't have an attachment to Dharma, nor does he have
an attachment to self. He has no attachment to self, no
attachment to Dharma, and also no attachment to emptiness.
He has no attachment to people, to self, or to emptiness.
This is the perfect clarity of samadhi and wisdom, without attachment to emptiness.

You may ask, "In explaining the word "aeon," since
you said that there is no past, present, or future,
then why do we still speak of the past, present, and
future?"

Didn't I just tell you? It's because, in their
minds, living beings have these thoughts of discrimination; that is why we talk about the past, present, and
future.

But just what is an "aeon." That's a complicated
question and we really don't have enough "time" to go
into it. Let's say that "one increasing and one decreasing constitute and aeon."

What is meant by "one increasing and one decreasing?"

"Decreasing" means that every hundred years, the
human lifespan decreases by one year and the average
height decreases by one inch. When human life expectancy
has decreased to ten years, it again begins to increase.
It increases in the same way, one year and one inch
every one hundred years, until human life expectancy
reaches eighty-four thousand years. At that point it
begins to decrease again. When it has decreased again
to eighty-thousand years, Maitreya Bodhisattva will
appear in the world as a Buddha. One cycle of increase
and decrease is called and aeon.

One thousand of these aeons is called a "small aeon."
One thousand small aeons is called a "middle-sized
aeon." Four middle-sized aeons make up a "great aeon."

Our world is divided into periods of becoming,
dwelling, decay, and emptiness. The becoming (creation)
of a world lasts for twenty small aeons. The period of
dwelling lasts for twenty small aeons. The periods of
decay and emptiness also last for twenty small aeons.
Therefore, within a great aeon is contained the complete cycle of becoming, dwelling, decay, and emptiness. That is what is called a great aeon.

And here in the text, how many great aeons are
we speaking of? An uncountable number. Why do I say
they are uncountable? Because they are beyond all
count; there is no way you could calculate their number.

INNUMERABLE EXTINCT BUDDHAS/ Within these countless
aeons, an unlimited number of Buddhas became Buddhas
and then entered Nirvana. This took a very long time.
HUNDREDS OF THOUSANDS OF MYRIADS OF MILLIONS OF THEM/
A NUMBER BEYOND ALL CALCULATION/ WORLD HONORED ONES
SUCH AS THESE/ USED VARIOUS CONDITIONS AND ANALOGIES/
expedient Dharma-doors/ AND THE POWER OF COUNTLESS
EXPEDIENTS/ TO PROCLAIM THE MARKS OF ALL DHARMAS/ They
proclaim the real mark of all dharmas.

There are one hundred dharmas, and also a thousand
dharmas, ten thousand dharmas, an unlimited number of
dharmas. What are the hundred dharmas? There are eleven
kinds of form dharmas, eight mind dharmas, fifty-one
dharmas belonging to the mind, twenty-four dharmas
not interacting with the mind, and six unconditioned
dharmas. A verse about the hundred dharmas goes:

Form dharmas are of eleven different kinds,
Eight kinds of dharmas are of the mind.
Fifty-one belong, twenty-four don't interact,
Plus six unconditioned make
one hundred in fact.

But all of these dharmas are spoken for the sake of
the Real Mark Dharma.

ALL OF THOSE WORLD HONORED ONES/ SPOKE THE DHARMA
OF ONE VEHICLE/ They all speak of the Buddha Vehicle,
the real wisdom. They open the provisional to reveal
the real. The Three Storehouse Teaching which they set
forth previously was to manifest the provisional for
the sake of the real. But their final destination is
to speak the wonderful doctrine of the Real Mark, in
other words the doctrines discussed in *The Wonderful
Dharma Lotus Flower Sutra*. TRANSFORMING BEINGS WITHOUT
LIMIT/ They teach and transform an unlimited number of
beings.

Sutra: (T.262, 8c8)

121-122
Further, all Great Sagely Lords,

Know the deep desires in the hearts

Of all the gods, humans, and other beings

Within all the worlds.

Using different expedients,

Which help to reveal the foremost principle.

123-125
If there are living beings

Who have met with Buddhas in the past

Heard the Dharma, practiced giving,

Morality, patience, and vigor

Dhyana samadhi, wisdom, and so on,

Cultivating blessings and wisdom,

Persons such as these

Have all realized the Buddha path.

Commentary:

FURTHER, ALL GREAT SAGELY LORDS/ all the Buddhas,
KNOW THE DEEP DESIRES IN THE HEARTS/ OF ALL THE GODS,
HUMANS, AND OTHER BEINGS/ WITHIN ALL THE WORLDS/ There
is the world of sentience and the material world. The
world of sentience is also called the Orthodox Retri-
bution World and the Dependent Retribution World.
USING DIFFERENT EXPEDIENTS/ THEY HELP TO REVEAL THE
FOREMOST PRINCIPLE/ Because they understand the thoughts
of desire of living beings, they set forth provisional,
clever, expedient device Dharma-doors to rescue living
beings. The expedients include the Sound Hearer Vehicle,
the Conditioned-Enlightened Vehicle, and the Bodhisattva
Vehicle.
IF THERE ARE LIVING BEINGS/ WHO HAVE MET WITH
BUDDHAS IN THE PAST/ in former lives, HEARD THE DHARMA,
PRACTICED GIVING/ MORALITY, PATIENCE, AND VIGOR/ DHYANA
SAMADHI, WISDOM, AND SO ON/ If any of the different kinds
of living beings listened to the Buddhadharma, to the
teaching of the Six Perfections, then they may have
decided to practice them. Giving is the first of the
Six Perfections. There are three kinds of giving: The
giving of wealth, the giving of the Dharma, and the
giving of fearlessness. Giving cures one of stinginess.

If you're a miser, you can't practice giving. If you practice giving, you can reduce your miserliness.

Morality, the second of the Six Perfections, cures one of bad conduct.

Patience, the third Perfection, crosses over anger. Do you like to lose your temper? You should cultivate the Perfection of Patience and not get angry. Change your attitude; change your temperament. When people with quick tempers refrain from getting angry, that is patience.

Vigor is the fourth perfection; it takes laxness across. Are you lazy? Cultivate vigor!

Dhyana samadhi, the fifth, cures one of scatteredness. Do you lack samadhi power? Then you should cultivate it. If you don't cultivate it, you'll never have it.

The last of the Six Perfections is that of wisdom. What does wisdom cross over? Stupidity. If you have wisdom, your stupidity will turn to wisdom; if you have no wisdom, your wisdom turns into stupidity. It's one thing, but it goes by two names. The other five Perfections work the same way. Patience is simply the transformation of anger. Vigor is the transformation of laziness. Dhyana samadhi is the transformation of scatteredness. It's just a matter of making the transformation. If you break precepts, but then keep them, you have transformed your precept-breaking into morality.

Giving is the transformation of stinginess. So you can't part with anything? It's just because you can't let go, that you can't obtain anything. If you want to "get," you first must give. If you don't give, you can't receive.

Stinginess: You really don't want to part with that money, do you? Giving money is like cutting off your own flesh. To part with a penny brings a pain to your heart and a pain to your liver.

The Six Perfections must be cultivated in order to realize Buddhahood.

CULTIVATING BLESSINGS AND WISDOM/ By practicing the Six Perfections, you cultivate blessings and wisdom. PERSONS SUCH AS THESE/ HAVE ALL REALIZED THE BUDDHA PATH. Figure it out. How long did it take them to practice the Six Perfections and the Ten Thousand Conducts in order to realize Buddhahood? In the beginning, they cultivated good on a small scale, but it continued to build up until it was a great amount of goodness. From one act of goodness, many acts of goodness grew.

From the cultivation of one blessing, many blessings
came to be cultivated. Then when both blessings and
wisdom were perfected, they accomplished Buddhahood.
     Now, we are beginning to cultivate. None of us
knows how many lives we have cultivated previously.
But no matter how many lifetimes one has been cultivating, whether one has, in fact, cultivated at all in
the past, one should still cultivate. You can't *not*
cultivate. You can't say, for example, "Since I didn't
cultivate in former lives, I might as well forget about
doing it now." That way, you'll *never* have any blessings
or wisdom. If you didn't cultivate in former lives,
you should start cultivating now. If you did cultivate
in former lives, you should continue to cultivate. You
shouldn't worry about whether or not you planted
blessings and wisdom in former lives. In this present
life we have encountered the supreme Buddhadharma,
and so we should certainly begin and be vigorous and
brave right up until we become Buddhas, at which time
we can consider our work finished.

Sutra: (T.262 8c15)

126
　When those Buddhas have become extinct

　If there are those with compliant hearts,

　Beings such as these

　Have attained the Buddha Way.

127
　After the extinction of those Buddhas,

　Those who have made offerings to their sharira,

　Building millions of kinds of stupas,

　Made of gold, silver, or of crystal,

　Mother-of-pearl, carnelian,

　Rose quartz, lapis lazuli, and other gems,

　Clear, pure and most ornate,

　Worked to grace the stupas,

　Or should there be those who've built temples

　Out of stone, chandana, or aloeswood,

　Hovenia, or other timbers,

　Bricks, clay, and the like,

　Or those who, in the barren wastes,

Have piled up earth into a Buddha-shrine,

Or even children who, at play,

Have piled up sand to make a stupa,

All persons such as these,

Have realized the Buddha Way.

Commentary:

WHEN THOSE BUDDHAS HAVE BECOME EXTINCT/ have
entered Nirvana, IF THERE ARE THOSE WITH COMPLIANT
HEARTS/ If they have brought forth gentle hearts and
are not head-strong, although at first glance it may
not look like they have many good roots, gradually they
will pile up merit and virtue. Eventually, after a
time BEINGS SUCH AS THESE/ HAVE ATTAINED THE BUDDHA
WAY/ They have already become Buddhas.

AFTER THE EXTINCTION OF THOSE BUDDHAS/ THOSE
WHO HAVE MADE OFFERINGS TO THEIR SHARIRA/ Those who
have built pagodas to contain the relics of the
Buddha so that offerings can be made to them, BUILDING
MILLIONS OF KINDS OF STUPAS/ Stupas to hold the relics
of the Buddhas should be thirteen stories high. Stupas
for Pratyeka Buddhas should be five stories high.
Stupas for fourth Stage Arhats should be four stories
high. Stupas for third stage Arhats should be three
stories high. Stupas for second stage Arhats should
be two stories high, and stupas for first stage Arhats
should be one story.

What are the stupas made out of? MADE OF GOLD,
SILVER, OR OF CRYSTAL/ MOTHER-OF-PEARL, CARNELIAN/
ROSE QUARTZ, LAPIS LAZULI, AND OTHER GEMS/ CLEAR, PURE
AND MOST ORNATE/ WORKED TO GRACE THE STUPAS/ The gems
are intertwined and hang in chains around the top of
the stupas.

OR SHOULD THERE BE THOSE WHO'VE BUILT TEMPLES/
OUT OF STONE, CHANDANA, OR ALOESWOOD/ HOVENIA OR OTHER
TIMBERS/ BRICKS, CLAY, AND THE LIKE/ OR THOSE WHO, IN
THE BARREN WASTES/ HAVE PILED UP EARTH INTO A BUDDHA-
SHRINE/ OR EVEN CHILDREN, WHO, AT PLAY/ HAVE PILED UP
SAND TO MAKE A STUPA/ ALL PERSONS SUCH AS THESE/
HAVE REALIZED THE BUDDHA WAY/ All of these different
kinds of people have accumulated a vast amount of
merit and virtue. They all become Buddhas.

Sutra: (T.262, 8c26)

128 Those who, for the Buddhas,
     Have erected images,
     Carving all their myriads of marks,
     Have realized the Buddha Way.
     They may have used the seven gems,
     Or bronze or copper, white or red,
     Wax, lead, or tin,
     Iron, wood, or clay,
     Or, perhaps, lacquered cloth,
     In making Buddha images;
     Persons such as these
     Have realized the Buddha Way.

Commentary:

THOSE WHO, FOR THE BUDDHAS/ HAVE ERECTED IMAGES/ Those who, as an offering to the Buddhas, have made images, by CARVING ALL THEIR MYRIADS OF MARKS/ all of the fine characteristics of the Buddhas of the ten directions. HAVE REALIZED THE BUDDHA WAY/ They have become Buddhas.

THEY MAY HAVE USED THE SEVEN GEMS/ gold, silver, lapis lazuli, crystal, mother-of-pearl, red pearls, or carnelian. OR BRONZE OR COPPER, WHITE OR RED/ WAX, LEAD, OR TIN/ IRON, WOOD, OR CLAY/ OR, PERHAPS, LACQUERED CLOTH/ IN MAKING BUDDHA-IMAGES/ PERSONS SUCH AS THESE/ there are eleven kinds of meritorious virtues derived from making Buddha images:

1. In every life you will have clear vision.
2. You will not be born in evil palces. Your friends and neighbors will all be good people. You won't meet up with evil people or evil beasts.
3. You'll always be born in a noble family. You will be born into a household which is wealthy and honored.
4. Your body will be purple-golden in color.
5. You'll possess an abundance of wealth.
6. You will be born in a worthy and good family.
7. You can be born a king. Now, there is no Emperor, but you could be the President. It amounts to

the same thing. Or, if you insist on being an Emperor,
you can find a country with a monarchy and be born
there.

8. You can be a Wheel-Turning Sage King. That's
even higher than being President. As a Wheel-Turning
Sage King, if you cultivate, you can become a Buddha.

9. You can be born in the Brahma Heavens and live
for an aeon. You can be a king among the gods.

10. You will not fall into the evil paths. Those
who make Buddha images will not fall into the hells,
the animal realm, or the realm of hungry ghosts.

11. In future incarnations you will still be able
to revere the Triple Jewel. You will be able to take
refuge with the Triple Jewel. You will not fall.

Hearing these eleven meritorious virtues, if we
have the strength, we should make more Buddha images.
If you make Buddha images, your appearance will be
perfect and full. Why is the Buddha's appearance so
perfect? It's because during the three great asankhyeya
aeons he cultivated the Way, he made countless Buddha
images. During the first asankhyeya aeon, he encountered
75,000 Buddhas. During the second, 76,000, and during
the third, 77,000. If he met with that many Buddhas, of
course he made more Buddha images than that. Who knows
how many he made? That is why his appearance is so
full and perfect. But, in making images, we shouldn't
think, "I'll make a Buddha image and then I will be
very handsome, and people will fall in love with me."
That's not a proper motive. We should cultivate blessings
and wisdom so that in the future we can realize Buddhahood.

Persons who have made such images have all realized
Buddhahood.

Sutra: (T.262, 9a2)

129 Those who painted bright Buddha images,

   Adorned with the marks of their hundreds of blessings,

   Whether they did it themselves or employed others,

   Have realized the Buddha Way.

   Even children who, at play,

   Who with a straw, a stick, or pen,

   Or even with their fingernails,

   Drew images of the Buddha,

   People such as these,

Gradually accumulated merit and virtue,

Perfected the heart of great compassion,

And have realized the Buddha Way.

They teach only Bodhisattvas,

And rescue countless multitudes.

Commentary:

Although previously the text said that one may make Buddha images out of lacquered cloth, the precepts discourage the use of lacquer, as it has an unpleasant

The precepts also say that one is not allowed to sit in front of a standing Buddha image or recline in front of a sitting Buddha image.

THOSE WHO PAINTED BRIGHT BUDDHA IMAGES/ ADORNED WITH THE MARKS OF THEIR HUNDREDS OF BLESSINGS/ The Buddha images are adorned with the many blessed marks of the Buddhas. WHETHER THEY DID IT THEMSELVES OR EMPLOYED OTHERS/ HAVE REALIZED THE BUDDHA WAY/ They have all become Buddhas.

EVEN CHILDREN WHO, AT PLAY/ WHO WITH A STRAW, A STICK, OR PEN/ Perhaps they draw a Buddha images with a straw, or with a stick of wood, or perhaps they draw one with a color crayon. OR EVEN WITH THEIR FINGERNAILS/ Or perhaps, playing in the mud, they traced out a Buddha image with their fingernails. DREW IMAGES OF THE BUDDHA/ Long ago, in Szechwan, there was a person who recited *The Vajra Sutra*. As he recited it, he would write it out in empty space with his hand. He stood in the same place everyday and recited and "wrote it out" in this way. Later, when it rained, the rain didn't fall in the spot where he had written out the Sutra. This happened everytime it rained. Those who had opened their Buddha Eyes saw that, even though the man had written out the Sutra in empty space, the gods and dragons and the eight-fold division were there protecting the Sutra and not allowing the rain to fall on that spot. Later a temple was built there. So you see, all he did was write it out in the air with his hand and he received such a great response. This really happened. It is recorded in a work entitled *The Efficacious Events of the Vajra Sutra*.

PEOPLE SUCH AS THESE/ mentioned above GRADUALLY ACCUMULATED MERIT AND VIRTUE/ PERFECTED THE HEART OF GREAT COMPASSION/ AND HAVE REALIZED THE BUDDHA WAY. They have realized supreme enlightenment.

Sutra: (T.262, 9a10)

130 Should persons, in stupas or in temples,
Make offerings with a reverent heart,
To jewelled or painted images,
With flowers, incense, banners, or canopies,
Or should they cause others to make music,
With drums, horns, or conches,
Pan-pipes, flutes, lutes or bamboo lyres,
Guitars, cymbals, or brass gongs,
With many wondrous sounds as these,
Played solely as offerings...

Commentary:

SHOULD PERSONS, IN STUPAS OR IN TEMPLES/ MAKE
OFFERINGS WITH A REVERENT HEART/ TO JEWELLED OR PAINT-
ED IMAGES/ WITH FLOWERS, INCENSE, BANNERS, OR CANOPIES/
If, holding thoughts of respect, they make offerings
to Buddha images of incense, banners, canopies, or
other articles such as beads, clothing, food and drink,
or merely place their palms together...
OR SHOULD THEY CAUSE OTHERS TO MAKE MUSIC/ Perhaps
they invite other people to make music WITH DRUMS,
HORNS, OR CONCHES/ PAN-PIPES, FLUTES, LUTES OR BAMBOO
LYRES/ GUITARS, CYMBALS, OR BRASS GONGS/ all different
kinds of musical instruments. Brass gongs are rather
large. Perhaps you've never seen any.
When you are making music before the Buddha
you should make proper music. You must not sing
love songs, songs about men and women. Your music must
be in praise of the Triple Jewel. Hitting the wooden
fish and ringing small bells is a kind of music-making.
Reciting Sutras and mantras is also a kind of
musical offering.
WITH MANY WONDROUS SOUNDS AS THESE/ PLAYED SOLELY
AS OFFERINGS/ All these subtle and wonderful sounds
are offered to the Buddha.

Sutra: (T.262, 9a15)

Or if, with happy hearts, with songs
And chants they praised the Buddha's virtues,

With even just one small sound,
They have realized the Buddha Way.
If people with scattered minds
Have given but a single flower
As an offering to a painted image,
They shall gradually see numberless Buddhas.
If they bowed in worship,
Or merely placed their palms together,
Or even raised a single hand,
Or gave a slight nod of the head,
As an offering to the images,
They shall gradually see countless Buddhas,
And have, themselves, realized the Buddha Way.
They will rescue countless multitudes,
And enter Nirvana without residue,
As a fire goes out when the fuel has been consumed.

Commentary:

OR IF, WITH HAPPY HEARTS, WITH SONGS/ AND CHANTS THEY PRAISED THE BUDDHA'S VIRTUES/ Chants are "Brahma" or pure sounds, like odes. They laud the virtues of the Buddha, praising his virtue in the Way. WITH EVEN JUST ONE SMALL SOUND/ Maybe they make only a tiny melody. THEY HAVE REALIZED THE BUDDHA WAY/ If, by means of a very small sound they accomplish the Buddha Path, they will accomplish the Path even quicker with more and bigger sounds!

IF PEOPLE WITH SCATTERED MINDS/ If there are people who have no samadhi power and who are confused, but who HAVE GIVEN BUT A SINGLE FLOWER/ AS AN OFFERING TO A PAINTED IMAGE/ THEY SHALL GRADUALLY SEE NUMBERLESS BUDDHAS/ Because of the merit and virtue obtained by making such offerings, they will get to meet with an uncountable number of Buddhas.

IF THEY BOWED IN WORSHIP/ OR MERELY PLACED THEIR PALMS TOGETHER/ as a gesture of respect, OR EVEN RAISED A SINGLE HAND/ OR GAVE A SLIGHT NOD OF THE HEAD/ AS AN OFFERING TO THE IMAGES/ THEY SHALL GRADUALLY SEE COUNT-LESS BUDDHAS/ From that first thought of respect which inspired them to make even these very small gestures of worship, they will aquire merit and virtue. AND HAVE

THEMSELVES, REALIZED THE BUDDHA WAY/ THEY WILL RESCUE
COUNTLESS MULTITUDES/ Not only will they accomplish the
Buddha Path, but they will save countless living beings.
AND ENTER NIRVANA WITHOUT RESIDUE/ AS A FIRE GOES OUT
WHEN THE FUEL HAS BEEN CONSUMED/ When the firewood has
all been burned, the fire goes out. The living beings
with potential to be taught are like the fuel. The
Response Body of the Buddha which appears to rescue
living beings is like the fire. When the living beings
have all been crossed over, the "response" fire goes
out.

Sutra: (T.262, 9a24)

131 If people with scattered minds,

Enter stupas or temples,

And say but once, "Namo Buddha,"

They have realized the Buddha Way.

Commentary:

IF PEOPLE WITH SCATTERED MINDS/ "Scattered" means
that they have no samadhi power, they are not at all
concentrated. These lines describe a situation such
as when the tourists come here to visit the temple
and gaze around at the Buddha images. They do not have
sincere hearts. What is more, they may look at the images
but they don't know anything at all about the Buddha.
You could say they were the scattered ones among the
scattered ones.
ENTER STUPAS OR TEMPLES/ If they go into Buddhist
stupas or Buddhist temples, AND SAY BUT ONCE, "NAMO
BUDDHA"/ All they have to do is say one sentence,
"Homage to the Buddha." From that one recitation, they
will ultimately realize Buddhahood.
Why is this? It's because "a journey of a thousand
miles begins with a single step." If you want to travel
a thousand miles, where do you begin? You begin with
the first step. Having taken that first step, you can
travel a thousand miles. "The perfect interpenetration
of the myriad virtues begins with the first thought."
If you wish to become a Buddha, it begins with that
very first thought, In that first thought, you plant
the Buddha seed; in the future, you reap the fruit of
Buddhahood.
Reciting "Namo Buddha," "Namo Amitabha Buddha," or
"Namo Shakyamuni Buddha," or "Namo Medicine Master Buddha

Who Dispels Calamities and Lengthens Life," may seem
very easy to do, but such an opportunity is not easy
to meet up with. All of you know how to recite the
Buddha's name, but think it over: Of all the people in
the world, are those who do not know how to recite the
Buddha's name in the majority or are those who do? You
might say that those who know how to recite are as few
as the moon and those who do not know how to recite are
as many as the stars. Are there more stars or more
moons? Those who can recite the Buddha's name are able
to do so because the good roots from their former lives
have matured enabling them to encounter the Dharma-door
of Buddha Recitation.

When the Buddha was in the world, he had a cousin
named Devadatta. Devadatta was the Buddha's enemy. He
did nothing but oppose the Buddha. The Buddha taught his
disciples to eat one meal a day, in the middle of the
day, but Devadatta was determined to out-do him. "So
you eat one meal a day?" he said, "I teach my disciples
to eat one meal every hundred days!" Shakyamuni Buddha
taught his disciples to be vegetarians and not to eat
meat. Devadatta said, "Not only do I teach my disciples
to refrain from eating meat, they don't even consume
salt." This was done merely to prove that, no matter
what, Devadatta was always higher than the Buddha. But
no matter how hard he tried, he never could recite the
Buddha's name. If you tried to teach him to recite, he
would refuse to do it. All his life, all he ever did
was commit offenses, continually opposing the Buddha.
When his evil karma had finally reached the point of
overflowing, he went to hell, alive. Going to hell
alive means that, in his very body of flesh he went to
hell. Just as he was about to go to hell, just as he was
at the gates of hell, he thought to recite the Buddha's
name. He wanted to recite it, but he couldn't get a
sound out. All he could scream was "Namo!" He couldn't
say the word "Buddha." His karmic obstacles bound him
up so tightly that he couldn't say the Buddha's name.
Shakyamuni Buddha saw him and said, "He's really pitiful, but don't look on him lightly. When he's finished
his punishment in the hells, he will become a Pratyeka
Buddha. His Buddha name will be simply "Namo." Because
he recited "Namo" as he fell into hell, as a Pratyeka
Buddha, he will be called "Namo."

So don't look on it as all so easy and think, "I
can recite the Buddha's name whenever I feel like it."
Right now, you aren't blocked by your karmic obstacles.
When they obstruct you, if you tried to recite it, you
wouldn't be able to do so.

There is another story about reciting the Buddha's
name: When the Buddha was in the world, there was a
very poor, old man. He saw Shakyamuni Buddha, accompanied by his 1250 disciples going out every day to beg for
food, and he thought it was not bad. Every day they went
out with their bowls, begged for food, came back and
ate, and that was all there was to it. "Very well," he
thought, "I'll leave home." He thought the Bhikshus
were very comfortable and didn't have to do any work,
so bitterness and no bother, very pure and free
So he decided to leave home and went to the Jeta Grove
to ask for permission to do so. But that day the Buddha
had gone out to accept offerings of food for lunch. As
for the Buddha's disciples, some had opened their Buddha
Eyes, some had opened their Wisdom Eyes, some had
opened their Dharma Eyes, and some had the Five Eyes and
the Six Spiritual Penetrations. Others had certified to
the first, second, third, and fourth stages of Arhatship.

Now, to "open" the eyes is not to certify to the
fruit. When people have opened their Buddha Eye, this
is called "the penetration obtained from virtue." This
happens because, in previous lives; one has cultivated
the Forty-Two Hands and the Shurangama Mantra a great
deal. These Dharma-doors bring about that reward. But
this is definitely not the same as certifying to the
first fruit, the second, third, or fourth fruit.
Arhats who have certified to the fruit can see the
operation of cause and effect throughout eighty
thousand great aeons. Those who have opened their
Buddha Eye or their Wisdom Eye may be able to see as
far as one life, two lives, three lives, five lives,
ten lives, one hundred lives, a thousand lives, or ten
thousand lives, but they cannot see as far as eighty
thousand great aeons.

Certified Arhats, however, can see all the causes
and effects of eighty thousand great aeons. When the
poverty-stricken old man came to leave the home-life,
the Disciples, the Great Arhats, contemplated and
observed his potential to see if he was fit to leave
home. They saw that this person, in the last eighty
thousand great aeons, had never made an offering to
the Buddha, had never bowed to the Buddha, had never
recited the Buddha's name or uttered even a tiny sound
of praise as an offering to the Buddha or a single
flower, or even put his hands together, or waved his
hand, or even nodded his head! Since he had no merit
and virtue, how could he leave home? It is said:

Don't say that leaving home is easy to do;
It's the result of planting the causes of
        Bodhi throughout many lives.
  Those who leave home must have planted good roots
in many lives and brought forth the Bodhi-heart. It's
not just a matter of thinking, "I'd like to leave home,"
and doing it. If you don't have the good roots, you
might want to leave home, but obstacles will arise. You
might leave home for one or two days and then return to
lay-life. You might leave home for one or two years,
for three, five, or ten years, and then return to lay-
life and not leave home again. Such things do happen.
So, don't think leaving home is very simple.
  So that Arhats saw that he had not planted good
roots in the last eighty great aeons and therefore would
not be able to leave home. They told him, "You can't
leave home. You are too old; you can't cultivate. It
would be best for you to go back to where ever you
came from. Don't stay here."
  Hearing this, the old man was overcome with grief.
On the one hand he walked, and on the other he thought,
"I thought leaving home would be very simple. I never
would have guessed that the Buddha's disciples would
refuse me. Probably they won't accept me because I am
old and poor. Well, if they won't accept me, I'll just
go jump in the sea and drown and end it all!" Then, still
walking and weeping, he made his way for the sea and
suicide. But, just as he was about to jump, along
came Shakyamuni Buddha, who said, "Old man, why are you
throwing yourself in the sea?"
  "I wanted to leave home," the old man replied.
"I went to the Jeta Grove to do so, but the Buddha
wasn't there, and the Buddha's Disciples wouldn't accept
me. As far as I'm concerned, there is really nothing
joyful in human existence; I'd rather just hurry up and
end my life. My life is meaningless."
  Shakyamuni Buddha said, "So you want to leave
home? That's no problem. Come back with me. I'll allow
you to leave home."
  The old man returned with the Buddha, left home,
cultivated, and after just a few days, certified to the
fruit of Arhatship. The Buddha's Disciples did not
understand this at all. "How strange!" they thought.
"This person has no good roots; how could he certify to
Arhatship? He hasn't done a single good deed throughout
the last eighty thousand great aeons. How could the
Buddha permit him to leave home?" They questioned the
Buddha and the Buddha gave them this explanation:

"You Arhats can only see the causes and effects of the last eighty thousand great aeons. What happened outside of that, you don't know. This old man, over eighty thousand aeons ago, was a poor firewood gatherer in the mountains. One day, he met up with a tiger. Just as the tiger was about to bite him, in his great fear he screamed, "Namo Buddha!" That one recitation scared the tiger away, and so he wasn't eaten. The seed planted by his single recitation of "Namo Buddha" has now matured as the good roots which have enabled him to leave home and certify to the fruit of Arhatship.

From the looks of this we can tell that it is not easy to leave home.

Also, in India there was a certain outside Way sect whose members made offerings to the image of a heavenly spirit. The heavenly spirit's body was made of wood or clay, but the head was made of gold. Once a thief wanted to steal the head, but when he went to take it, the awesome virtue of the heavenly spirit made him afraid. In his fear, he thought to recite, "Namo Buddha!" The recitation dispelled his fears because it had stripped the heavenly spirit of its awesome virtue. Fearlessly, then, he stole off with the golden head. Later on everyone said, "Take a look at that heavenly spirit everyone believes in ." They said , "It's not the least bit efficacious. If it were, how could it have had its head stolen? It's useless to believe in it." When they said this, the heavenly spirit came alone and took possession of a person's body. Sometimes spirits give off an efficacious energy, and if it takes possession of someone, the victim will become senseless, as if they were drunk.

The spirit began to speak through the medium and said, "It's not that I am not efficacious. When the thief came, he was afraid to take my head. But when he recited "Namo Buddha" the whole area was flooded with Buddha-light and I couldn't even open my eyes. I was unable to protect my head. That's how he managed to steal it. It is certainly not the case that I am not efficacious, but the awesome virtue of the Buddha is even greater than mine, and so I had no way to protect my head."

Hearing this, one may wonder, "Did the Buddha assist the thief in stealing the golden head of the heavenly spirit? Did he aid him in doing this evil karma?" No. The thief recited the Buddha's name, and the merit and virtue that comes from reciting the Buddha's name is inconceivable. Whether a good person or an evil person recites, it has the same effect. It's

not the case that when an evil person recites it,
there is no merit and virtue, but when a good person
recites, there is. The merit and virtue is the same. So
even though he was a thief, he still called on the
Buddha and his recitation enabled him to steal the
heavenly spirit's gold head. The Buddha certainly wasn't
helping him be a thief. Rather, he was helping him
perfect his good roots.

You say, "If he steals, how can he have good roots?"
Take a look at this line of *The Dharma Flower Sutra:*
        "...and say but once, 'Namo Buddha,'
        They have realized the Buddha Way."
Even though, at that time, he was a thief, he
planted good roots through his recitation and so in
the future he can certainly become a Buddha. This is
called "vigor in opposition and in accord." Even though
he was a thief, he still recited the Buddha's name. The
Buddha didn't help him steal the heavenly spirit's head,
but the Buddha does treat everyone equally. Those who
recite, be they good or evil, obtain the same efficacious reponse.

Hearing this, you shouldn't make the mistake of
thinking"If the thief recited the Buddha's name and
stole the heavenly spirit's head, I'll go recite the
Buddha's name and steal perhaps the earth spirit's
silver head, or maybe some valuable human head!" You
can't get away with this. The thief who stole the
heavenly spirit's head knew nothing about the Buddhadharma. Perhaps he had heard someone say in passing,
"It's good to recite the Buddha's name," and so, when
he was afraid, it occurred to him to recite it. He had
certainly never studied the Buddhadharma. Students of
the Buddhadharma should take care not to use the
awesome virtue of Buddha-recitation or lean on the
Buddha's light to help them steal with impunity. You
cannot do that. Once you have studied the Buddhadharma
and know that stealing is against the law, if you go
ahead and do it, your offense is doubled. This is something you should all understand clearly. Why do I
bring this up? Because there was once a monk, who,
before leaving home had been in the army. Later,
he studied the Buddhadharma and had great faith in
Buddha-recitation. Before he left home he, himself,
recited, and he led others in recitation. Five or six
years after he left home he ran off to Tao Feng Mountain in Hong Kong, where they specialize in convincing
those who have left home to return to lay-life.

When the monk got there he took a job as a cook.
Those who left home always went off their vegetarian

diet when they went there. As cook, the monk thought
that because he recited the Buddha's name, he could
save the living beings as he killed them. So, as he
cut off chickens' heads he would recite "Namo Amitabha
Buddha." He thought that by reciting he could cross
the chickens over as he killed them, but in the end,
when he had been there for a little over half a year,
he went insane and died. So you cannot do this kind of
thing. Everyone should be particularly clear about
it. If you deliberately violate a precept, the offense
is tripled. He had no authority to do such a thing.
It is true that reciting the Buddha's name will save
living beings. If you have the power so see that, as
you kill them, they are for sure being reborn in the
Land of Ultimate Bliss, that's one thing. But, if you
can't actually see it happen, if you don't have the
power, you cannot. You can't just say, "I am hoping
that they will be reborn in the Land of Ultimate Bliss."
That's not good enough. Hearing this account, don't
misunderstand it and think that as long as you recite
the Buddha's name, you can create offenses. Those who
recite the Buddha's name should not commit offenses.
They should be even better than they were before they
recited it. They should not commit the smallest
offense or make the slightest mistake.

I knew that monk personally. Later, he went insane.
When   went insane, he wanted to see me. He knew that
if he could see me, perhaps he would have some hope of
eradicating his offense-karma. But he never did get to
see me. He was called Hung-hui, and was a grand-
disciple of the Venerable Hsü-lao.

Sutra: (T.262, 9a26)

132 Be it from Buddhas of the past,

 While existent, or after their extinction,

 Those who have heard this Dharma,

 Have realized the Buddha Way.

3-134 The World Honored Ones of the future,

 Are limitless in number;

 All of these Thus Come Ones,

 Will also speak the Dharma of expedient devices.

 All of the Thus Come Ones,

 By means of limitless expedients,

135-136 Help all living beings
To enter the Buddha's non-outflow wisdom.
Of those who have heard the Dharma,
None will fail to become Buddhas.

Commentary:

        BEING IT FROM BUDDHAS OF THE PAST/ WHILE EXISTENT
OR AFTER THEIR EXTINCTION/ Perhaps they were in the
world or perhaps they had entered Nirvana THOSE WHO HAVE
HEARD THIS DHARMA/ If there are those who have heard
The Wonderful Dharma Lotus Flower Sutra, They HAVE ALREADY
REALIZED THE BUDDHA WAY/ because all Buddhas of the
past have spoken this Sutra, all Buddhas of the present
are speaking this Sutra, and all Buddhas of the future
will speak this Sutra All those who have heard its
wonderful Dharma have already accomplished the Buddha
Path. They have all become Buddhas.
        THE WORLD HONORED ONES OF THE FUTURE/ ARE LIMIT-
LESS IN NUMBER/ They cannot be counted. ALL OF THESE
THUS COME ONES/ WILL ALSO SPEAK THE DHARMA OF EXPEDIENT
DEVICES/ They will first speak the provisional teaching
and later return to the real teaching. ALL OF THE THUS
COME ONES/ in the ten directions BY MEANS OF LIMITLESS
EXPEDIENTS/ employing countless Dharma-doors HELP ALL
LIVING BEINGS/ TO ENTER THE BUDDHA'S NON-OUTFLOW
WISDOM/ They cause all living beings to obtain the
non-outflow wisdom of the Buddha.
        OF THOSE WHO HAVE HEARD THE DHARMA/ "Hearing this
Dharma" simply means hearing *The Wonderful Dharma Lotus
Flower Sutra*. NONE WILL FAIL TO BECOME BUDDHAS/ Of those
who have heard *The Wonderful Dharma Lotus Flower Sutra*, not
one of them will not, in the future, become a Buddha. So
we are now able to hear this Sutra, and in the future
each of us will have the opportunity to become Buddhas.
Several thousand years ago Shakyamuni Buddha gave us
all predictions of future Buddhahood. Therefore, we
who have the opportunity to hear this Sutra should not
take ourselves lightly. In the future you can become a
Buddha. You shouldn't think that reciting the Buddha's
name is such a simple thing to do. We recite the
Buddha's name once and don't find it difficult. And
why isn't it difficult? It's because our karmic offenses
are not all that deep. People with karmic obstacles may
want to recite the Buddha's name, but they are unable to
do so. They are obstructed by their karmic obstacles
and so they can't recite even if they want to. Take

Devadatta, for example. He could only recite "Namo."
His karmic obstacles were so heavy he couldn't say the
word "Buddha."

An event in China also took place which proves that
those with heavy karmic obstalces are unable to recite
the Buddha's name. In China, during the Southern Sung
Dynasty, there was a great minister by the name of
Ch'in Hui. He had a few good roots, and so he was very
intelligent and placed first as a *chuang-yüan*, or a top
scholar in the Imperial Examinations. But after he became an official, he grew envious of the worthy and
jealous of the talented. In this way, he created a
great deal of offense karma. One of his worst deeds was
to have Yao Fei murdered. The offense karma he had
created was extremely heavy. Because Earth Store Bodhisattva had a close affinity with him, he came to take
him across. He made a plan in advance, "I'll go there
and if I can just get him to recite the word 'Buddha'
I will release him of all of his offenses. Then Earth
Store Bodhisattva turned himself into a Bhikshu and
went to see Ch'in Hui.

Ch'in Hui was at the height of his political career,
a Prime Minister to the Emperor. When he saw the monk
approaching, he called to him and engaged him in a conversation. The monk exhorted him to recite the Buddha's
name, but he wouldn't do it. He said, "You really should
recite the Buddha's name, a man in your high position..."
but he refused to recite it.

"What use is recitation?" he said. He simply would
not say the world 'Buddha.' All Earth Store Bodhisattva
wanted him to do was to say the word "Buddha" once and
then he could free Ch'in Hui of his offenses, but Ch'in
Hui refused to say it. Then Earth Store Bodhisattva
manifested spiritual penetrations. He used his "whisk,"
--in the forty-two hands there is one called the White
Whisk Hand, isn't there? Those who have left home carry
them to brush away the mosquitoes--Anyway, Earth Store
Bodhisattva brushed him with his whisk and Ch'in Hui was
forced to kneel in front of him. He wanted to get up,
but try as he might, he couldn't do it. Then Earth
Store Bodhisattva held out his palm and said, "Tell me
what word it is that I'm writing on my palm," as he
wrote the word "Buddha." All Ch'in Hui had to do was
say, "That's the word Buddha," in order to be freed
of all his offense karma. But what do you think Ch'in
Hui did? His heavenly eloquence burst forth and he said,
"When young, I was a top scholar. Now I'm number-one
Imperial Scholar. Every piece of literature in the
country must first be shown to me. If I couldn't

even read that word, how could I have become the Prime
Minister? I can read that word, all right, but I won't
say it for you!" All he had to do was read it, but
he wouldn't do it. Seeing this, Earth Store Bodhisattva
realized, "Ah, his offense karma is indeed heavy. There's
really no way I can save him." Later, Ch'in Hui fell into
hell.

This proves that recitation of the Buddha's name is
no simple matter. Why should we ordinarily recite the
Buddha's name? In preparation for the time when our
lives come to an end, and we will need to do so.

"If we will need to recite when our lives are
coming to an end, why not just wait until then? Why
do we have to recite now?" you ask.

Everything is a question of habits. If you don't
do something as a rule, then when your life is drawing
to a close, you won't remember how to recite the Buddha's
name. That is why, now, in ordinary times, we should
learn how to recite and cultivate the Pure Land Dharma-
door. Then, when our lives are over, we can be reborn
in the Land of Ultimate Bliss.

"Why should we be reborn in the Land of Ultimate
Bliss?" you ask.

It's because of the vows made by Amitabha Buddha in
the causal ground when he was a Bhikshu named Fa Tsang,
"Dharma Treasury." He made forty-eight vows and said,
"After I have become a Buddha, of all the living beings
in the ten directions, if there is one who calls my
name, who recites my name as Amitabha Buddha, I shall
certainly guide them to my land. They can come to my
land and eventually realize Buddhahood. In my land the
people will be transformationally born from lotus
flowers and their bodies will be clear and pure."Because of the vows made by Amitabha Buddha, all living
beings now who cultivate the Dharma-door of Buddha-
recitation will find it the easiest of the Dharma-
doors.

In the Sutras it is said, "Of those beings in the
Dharma-ending age, not one in a million who cultivate
will obtain the Way. Only through the practice of the
recitation of the Buddha's name will they be reborn in
the Land of Ultimate Bliss and thereby be saved. Now
it is the Dharma-ending age, and it is appropriate for
all of us to recite the Buddha's name. In the West,
however, it is not the Dharma-ending age. You could say
it is the Right Dharma age. This is because the Buddhadharma has just been transmitted to the West and is just
beginning to flourish. Many Americans like to sit in

Dhyana meditation. This is a sign of the Right Dharma
age.

But the Dharma-door of Buddha-recitation can be
cultivated in the Right Dharma age, and it can also be
cultivated in the Dharma-ending age. The Dharma-door
of Buddha recitation can be cultivated during any
period at all. So, if you aren't making progress with
other methods of work, you can cultivate the Dharma-
door of Buddha-recitation.

Dhyana Master Yung Ming Shou said, "With Dhyana
and with the Pure Land, one is like a tiger with horns."
That is, if you investigate Dhyana and recite the
Buddha's name, you are like a tiger with a pair of
horns. "In this life, you're a teacher of people, and
in the future you can be a Buddhist patriarch." Therefore, genuine investigation of Dhyana is the same as
genuine investigation of the Pure Land. Those who
genuinely recite the Buddha's name are just genuine
cultivators of Dhyana.

To explain it at an even more basic level: Those
who genuinely uphold the precepts are just genuine cultivators of Dhyana. Those who genuinely investigate
Dhyana are just genuine upholders of the precepts. Those
who genuinely lecture on Sutras and speak the Dharma
may do nothing else, but they are nonetheless genuine
investigators of Dhyana. A few days ago I said,

"Penetration of the sect,
  Penetration of speech,
  Samadhi and wisdom are perfect and clear,
  And there is no attachment to emptiness."

To be able to investigate Dhyana and also to
lecture on the Sutras is called penetration of both
the sect and speech, for one understands both the
practice of meditation and the method of lecturing on
the Sutras. To speak even more deeply: Those who genuinely investigate Dhyana are just genuine holders of
mantras. Those who are genuine holders of mantras, true
cultivators of the Secret School, are just genuine
cultivators of Dhyana. The five schools of Buddhism,
Dhyana, the Teachings, the Vinaya, the Secret, and
the Pure Land Schools, although they are said to be
five, are fundamentally the same, ultimately one,
non-dual. Not only are they one, but there isn't even
the "one." If there isn't even the "one" how could
there be five? Those who truly study the Buddhadharma
should understand this point. Some people say, "The
Dharma-door of Buddha recitation is the highest and the
Dharma-door of investigating Dhyana is incorrect."
Others say the opposite. This shows that they do not

understand the Buddhadharma. For those who truly understand the Buddhadharma, "all Dharmas are the Buddhadharma and none of them can be obtained." There isn't
any Dharma which can be obtained. Therefore, why add a
head on top of your head? Why look for trouble when
there isn't any? If you really understand the Dharma,
there is no Dharma which can be obtained. But, if you
tell people who don't understand the Buddhadharma,
"There isn't anything at all--nothing," they will feel
disappointed. That is why the Buddha spoke the provisional wisdom for the sake of the real wisdom, the
provisional Dharma for the sake of the real Dharma.
But in the end, what is the real wisdom like? It is
just "non-attainment;" it returns to the unobtainable.
The Real Mark is unmarked, and yet there is nothing
not marked by it. That is the true, real wisdom.

Sutra: (T.262, 9b4)

137
    All the Buddhas have made this vow

    "As to the Buddha Way which I have walked,

    I wish to lead all living beings

    Alike to obtain this Path."

138
    And although the Buddhas of the future

    Will speak a hundred thousand million,

    Countless Dharma-doors,

    They are, in fact, for the sake of One Vehicle.

    All Buddhas, Doubly Perfect Honored Ones,

    Know the Dharmas are eternally without a nature.

    The Buddha-seed arises from conditions;

    Thus they speak of the One Vehicle.

139
    This Dharma abides in the Dharma's position,

    Dwelling forever in worldly marks.

    Having understood this in the Bodhimanda,

    The Guiding Master teaches it expediently.

Commentary:

    The previous passage of text read, "All of the
Thus Come Ones/ By means of limitless expedients/ Help
all living beings/ To enter the Buddha's non-outflow

wisdom./ Of those who have heard this Dharma/ None will fail to become Buddhas./ This section of text falls under the heading of "the singularity of the cultivators." The present section of text: "All the Buddhas have made this vow/ As to the Buddha Way which I have walked/ I wish to lead all living beings/ Alike to obtain this Path.'/ falls under the outline heading of "the singularity of the practice."

The Dharma Flower Sutra contains the Ten Wonders of the Root and the Ten Wonders of the Branches. Presently we are discussing 1) the singularity of the cultivators, 2) the singularity of the practice, 3) the singularity of the teaching, and 4) the singularity of the principle.

So the Buddhas all made a vow to lead living beings to obtain the Way that they themselves walked down. You may ask, "Since there is no Dharma which can be obtained, why does the text say 'obtain the Way?'"

In *The Vajra Sutra,* Subhuti says, "While the Buddha was with Burning Lamp Buddha, there was no Dharma which he obtained as anuttarasamyak sambodhi." Anuttarasamyak sambodhi is possessed by us inherently. It is not obtained from the outside. That is why there is, in reality, nothing obtained.

We have it all along; it's just that we don't know that we do. Because we don't know we have it, it can be likened to a bright gem hidden in our clothing. We don't know that a shining gem has been sewn into our clothing. The gem is just the Buddha nature. We are basically one with the Buddha nature. Why haven't we become Buddhas? It's because we have not found our inherent Buddha nature within ourselves. We now want to become Buddhas, but this actually means getting back the valuables which were ours to begin with, nothing more. The text says, "Alike to obtain this Path." The Buddhas wish to lead all living beings to cultivate this Dharma-door. This shows the singularity of the practice.

AND ALTHOUGH THE BUDDHAS OF THE FUTURE/ all the Buddhas of the future WILL SPEAK A HUNDRED THOUSAND MILLION/ COUNTLESS DHARMA-DOORS/ THEY ARE, IN FACT, FOR THE SAKE OF ONE VEHICLE/ the Buddha Vehicle.

ALL BUDDHAS, DOUBLY PERFECT HONORED ONES/ those perfect in blessings and in wisdom KNOW THE DHARMAS ARE ETERNALLY WITHOUT A NATURE/ THE BUDDHA-SEED ARISES FROM CONDITIONS/ THUS THEY SPEAK OF THE ONE VEHICLE/ The Buddha's Dharma-doors arise from conditions. It is for the sake of the Buddha's teaching of the One Vehicle that all of other teachings are spoken, that is, the Storehouse Teaching, the Pervasive Teaching, and the

Separate Teaching. They are all really presented for
the sake of the Buddha Vehicle. This is to show the
singularity of the teaching. They are all for the
sake of the One Buddha Vehicle; there are no other
vehicles.
     THIS DHARMA ABIDES IN THE DHARMA'S POSITION/ "This
Dharma" refers to the Wonderful Dharma of *The Wonderful
Dharma Lotus Flower Sutra*. And where is the Dharma's
position? DWELLING FOREVER IN WORLDLY MARKS/ The Dharma
is found to dwell in worldly appearances, for in worldly
dharmas themselves are transcendental Dharmas found.
Transcendental Dharmas themselves are just worldly
dharmas. So the Sixth Patriarch said,
          "The Buddhadharma is in the world.
          Enlightenment is not apart from the world.
          To search for Bodhi apart from the world
          Is like looking for a hare with horns."
     HAVING UNDERSTOOD THIS IN THE BODHIMANDA/ Shakya-
muni Buddha says, "I sat in the field of enlightenment,
and, after I became a Buddha, I understood this doctrine. THE GUIDING MASTER TEACHES IT EXPEDIENTLY/ The
Guiding Master, the Buddha, uses all kinds of expedient devices to teach this Dharma. That is the
singularity of the principle. The essential principle
is one.

Sutra: (T.262, 9b12)

140 Those who receive the offerings of gods and humans,

     The Buddhas of the present in the ten directions,

     Their number like the Ganges' sands,

     Manifest within the world

     To bring peace and comfort to living beings,

     And also speak Dharma such as this.

     Knowing the foremost still extinction,

     They use the power of expedients

     To demonstrate the various paths,

     In reality, for the sake of the Buddha Vehicle.

     Knowing the conduct of living beings,

     The thoughts deep within their minds,

     Their habitual actions in the past,

     The nature of their desire, the power of their vigor,

And their faculties, keen or dull,

They employ various causes and conditions,

Analogies and verbal expressions,

To teach them the appropriate expedients.

Commentary:

THOSE WHO RECEIVE THE OFFERINGS OF GODS AND HUMANS/ those who are worthy of the offerings of the gods and of human beings, THE BUDDHAS OF THE PRESENT IN THE TEN DIRECTIONS/ all the Buddhas currently in the ten directions THEIR NUMBER LIKE THE GANGES' SANDS/ Their number is as many as the grains of sand in the Ganges River. MANIFEST WITHIN THE WORLD/ They appear in the worlds of the ten directions. TO BRING PEACE AND COMFORT TO LIVING BEINGS/ They act out of the desire to bring peace and security to living beings. AND ALSO SPEAK DHARMA SUCH AS THIS/ They also speak *The Wonderful Dharma Lotus Flower Sutra*. KNOWING THE FOREMOST STILL EXTINCTION/ knowing the number one Dharma of still extinction, the wonderful principle of the Real Mark, THEY USE THE POWER OF EXPEDIENTS/ If they started out by speaking the Real Mark, no one would understand, and so they use the power of various expedients and bestow the provisional for the sake of the real. TO DEMONSTRATE THE VARIOUS PATHS/ They set forth all manner of Dharma-doors and various expedient devices. IN REALITY, FOR THE SAKE OF THE BUDDHA VEHICLE/ They set them forth, in fact, for the sake of the One Buddha Vehicle. Their final aim, the ultimate goal, is to speak the Buddha Vehicle, to cause living beings to become Buddhas.

KNOWING THE CONDUCT OF LIVING BEINGS/ the actions of living beings, THE THOUGHTS DEEP WITHIN THEIR MINDS/ just what they are thinking, THEIR HABITUAL ACTIONS IN THE PAST/ the defilements habitually practiced in past lives, now present as karmic retribution, THE NATURE OF THEIR DESIRES, THE POWER OF THEIR VIGOR/ They all have thoughts of desire and a different measure of vigor in their cultivation. AND THEIR FACULTIES, KEEN OR DULL/ Some living beings have sharp dispositions and others are slow-witted. Those with keen faculties are intelligent. Those with dull faculties are stupid. THEY EMPLOY VARIOUS CAUSES AND CONDITIONS/ they use all types of causes and conditions, ANALOGIES AND VERBAL EXPRESSIONS/ parables and phrases TO TEACH THEM THE APPROPRIATE EXPEDIENTS/ According to the basic natures of living beings, they respond to them and

teach them the Dharma, using expedient devices. For
example, to living beings who are very stubborn, they
speak about compassion and in this way take them across.
They explain Prajna wisdom to stupid living beings so
that they may give rise to wisdom. They teach scattered
living beings how to cultivate Dhyana samadhi. To those
who are lax they teach vigor. Living beings who continually violate the precepts are instructed in morality. People heavily burdened with greed are taught to
give. They employ various expedient devices to teach
living beings. This is what is meant by, "To teach
them the appropriate expedients."

Sutra: (T.262, 9b21)

141-143 Now I, too, am like them.

Using various Dharma-doors,

I proclaim the Buddha Way

To bring peace and comfort to living beings.

144

I use the power of my wisdom,

To know the nature of beings' desires;

I speak all dharmas expediently,

To lead them all to happiness.

145-146 Shariputra, you should know,

As I regard them with my Buddha-eye,

I see living beings in the six paths,

Impoverished, lacking blessings and wisdom,

Entering the dangerous path of birth and death,

Where they suffer unremittingly.

They are deeply attached to the five desires,

Like a yak caring for its tail,

They smother themselves with greed and love,

Blind, and in darkness, seeing nothing.

They do not seek the mighty Buddha,

Or the Dharma which cuts off suffering,

But instead they deeply enter into deviant views;

With suffering, they wish to cast off suffering.

For the sake of these beings,

I give rise to the Great Compassion Heart.

Commentary:

NOW I, TOO, AM LIKE THEM/ Now, at present, I,
Shakyamuni Buddha, am also thus. I am like the Buddhas
of the past, future and present. USING VARIOUS DHARMA-
DOORS/ I PROCLAIM THE BUDDHA WAY/ TO BRING PEACE AND
COMFORT TO LIVING BEINGS/ I lead all living beings to
gain security and happiness.

I USE THE POWER OF MY WISDOM/ the Buddha's true,
real wisdom, TO KNOW THE NATURE OF BEINGS DESIRES/
All living beings have thier own particular natural
desires, the things they are fond of. I understand
them all very clearly. I SPEAK ALL DHARMAS EXPEDIENTLY/
Because I understand all living beings, I use expedient
Dharmas to teach and transform living beings, teaching
them all the dharmas. TO LEAD THEM ALL TO HAPPINESS/ I
lead all living beings to be filled with the true bliss
of Dharma, to receive the Dharma's moisture, as the
water moistens things. I moisten living beings with the
Dharma, to cause them to be filled with joy.

SHARIPUTRA, YOU SHOULD KNOW/ AS I REGARD THEM WITH
MY BUDDHA-EYE/ I SEE LIVING BEINGS IN THE SIX PATHS/
All of them, gods, humans, asuras, hell-beings, hungry
ghosts, and animals--IMPOVERISHED, LACKING BLESSINGS
AND WISDOM/ They are confused and deluded and don't
know how to wake up. This is because they have no wisdom
and no blessed retribution. Why not? Because they are
too poor. This is the poverty that results from not
understanding the Buddhadharma. They are truly pitiful,
truly poor. If they had blessings and wisdom, they
wouldn't be poor. But, because they have neither, they
are.

What is true wealth? Understanding the Buddhadharma is true wealth. What is poverty? Not understanding the Buddhadharma is poverty. Poverty and wealth
depend upon whether or not you have blessings and
wisdom. If you have blessings or wisdom, you are wealthy.
If you do not, you are poor.

Where do blessings and wisdom come from? They come
through cultivation of the Way. Therefore, the living
beings in the six paths are poor because they have no
blessings and no wisdom. ENTERING THE DANGEROUS PATH
OF BIRTH AND DEATH/ They enter the risky, evil road of
birth and death. The road of birth and death is extremely dangerous. It is said,

Having lost this human body,
In ten thousand aeons,it's hard to get another.
We are people at present, but don't think it is
easy to be a human being. Didn't I tell you earlier
that when Shakyamuni Buddha was in the world he once
picked up a handful of dirt and asked, "Is there more
dirt on the earth or more dirt in my hand?"

The Disciples all replied, "There is more dirt on
the earth than in the Buddha's hand."

The Buddha then said, "Those who obtain a human
body are like the dirt in my hand. Those who lose a
human body are like the dirt on the ground." So it is
extremely dangerous to enter the risky road of birth and
death.

WHERE THEY SUFFER UNREMITTINGLY/ Their suffering
continues from one life to the next. They may be a
human being in their present life, but there is no
guarantee that they will be one in their next life.
Their suffering is continuous and uninterrupted. The
causes of suffering, the result of suffering, the retribution of suffering--it simply never ends.

THEY ARE DEEPLY ATTACHED TO THE FIVE DESIRES/ Why
aren't they able to end their suffering? It's because
they are deeply enmeshed in the five desires, forms,
sounds, smells, tastes, and tangible objects, also
called the five "dusts," the five desires of the world.
LIKE A YAK CARING FOR ITS TAIL/ The yak is a kind of
ox that places great importance on its tail. Because it
thinks its tail is so important, it always watches out
for it. As a result, since it thinks its tail is so
important, people are always after it. Thus, out of its
great desire to protect its tail, it ends up losing its
very life. THEY SMOTHER THEMSELVES WITH GREED AND LOVE/
Smothering themselves, they die, like the yak. BLIND,
AND IN DARKNESS, SEEING NOTHING/ They are as if blind
and in darkness, so of course they cannot see. THEY
DO NOT SEEK THE MIGHTY BUDDHA/ They have no wisdom;
they do not seek a teacher who understands. Therefore,
those without wisdom are as if blind. If you have no
teacher, you are in the dark. You cannot see anything
at all. Not seeing the light means that you have no
wisdom. The Buddha has great power and can rescue all
living beings. OR THE DHARMA WHICH CUTS OFF SUFFERING/
They don't seek instruction from the Buddha in the
methods for cutting off suffering. BUT INSTEAD THEY
DEEPLY ENTER INTO DEVIANT VIEWS/ Because they don't
seek wisdom, they are like blindmen, they wander into
deviant views.

People are very strange. If you teach them the

Proper Dharma, you can teach until you are blue in the
face, but they won't understand it. One the other hand,
if you teach them a deviant dharma, they will catch on
after just one lesson. Wouldn't you say this was
strange? If it's the Proper Dharma, you can try to
teach them once, twice, three times, and they find it
difficult to remember. If you teach them some heretical
"occult" dharmas, they remember them very easily. People
believe the deviant dharmas. They may believe the
Proper Dharma for a moment, but they soon lose faith in
it. After awhile, as soon as your back is turned, they
no longer believe. So they "deeply enter into deviant
views."

Why is it so hard for people to learn Proper
Dharma, and so easy for them to learn deviant ones?
It's because, life after life, we have been deeply
enmeshed in deviant views. The deviant views are our
old friends, as familiar as our own blood relatives.
So it is easy to learn them. We have forgotten the
Proper Dharma. Although we study it, it's hard for us
to remember it. We learn it once, and then forget it,
learn it again and forget it again. Why do we forget
it? Because we have become separated from it by too
great a distance. We have grown farther and farther
away from it, and soon forget it altogether.

WITH SUFFERING, THEY WISH TO CAST OFF SUFFERING/
With their misery, with the root of their suffering,
they try to get rid of their suffering. This is
difficult to manage.

What is the root of suffering? Ignorance. It is
said,

> Ignorance and its various aspects
>   are the root of pain;
> When the root of pain has been cast out,
>   wholesome roots remain.
> Merely rely on the wisdom sword's
>   awesome spiritual might,
> To jump right off the spinning wheel,
>   and over the six-path gates.[1]

---

[1] 種種無明是苦根
　苦根去盡善根存
　但憑慧劍威神力
　跳出輪迴六道門

Ignorance is the root of suffering. When you cut off ignorance, you also cut off suffering at the root. If you wish to cut off ignorance, how are you going to do it? Merely make use of your wisdom sword. With the wisdom sword, you can cut off ignorance and jump right off the spinning wheel of rebirth. The most important thing is to have the wisdom sword. Without it, you won't be able to get out of the sea of suffering.

FOR THE SAKE OF THESE BEINGS/ Because the Buddha sees living beings sunk in the sea of suffering, being born and dying over and over again, never ending birth and death, the Buddha says, I GIVE RISE TO THE GREAT COMPASSION HEART/ The Buddha gives rise to a heart filled with compassion. How does the compassionate heart arise? The Buddha thinks, "Ah, these living beings are just like my own sons and daughters. How can a parent stand by and watch his children suffer?" He gives rise to a heart of great compassion to teach and transform living beings, to relieve them of their suffering and rescue them from the sea of misery.

Sutra: (T.262, 9c4)

147-149 When first I sat in the Bodhimanda,

In contemplation, or walking about the tree,

For a full three times seven days,

I thought over matters such as these:

The wisdom which I have obtained,

Is subtle, wonderful, and foremost,

150   But living beings are dull-rooted,

Attached to pleasure, blinded by delusion;

Beings such as these,

How can they possibly be saved?

151   Just then the Brahma Heaven Kings,

As well as the God Shakra,

The Four World-Protecting God Kings,

The god of the heaven of Great Comfort,

And the other heavenly multitudes,

With retinues numbering in the billions

Reverently placed their palms together,

And requested me to turn the Dharma Wheel.

I then thought to myself,

"Were I to praise only the Buddha Vehicle,

Beings sunk in suffering

Would be unable to believe this Dharma.

They would slander it out of disbelief,

And fall into the three evil paths.

It's better that I do not speak the Dharma,

But quickly enter into Nirvana."

Commentary:

WHEN I FIRST SAT IN THE BODHIMANDA/ Shakyamuni
Buddha says, "When I had just become a Buddha and
was sitting in the field of the Way...IN CONTEMPLATION,
OR WALKING ABOUT THE TREE/ After I became a Buddha, I
contemplated the past causes and conditions and also
the future causes and conditions. Sometimes I walked
around the tree. On the one hand, this was good exer-
cise, and on the other it served to bring the thoughts
of the heart together so that it did not become
scattered."

"The Buddha's heart is basically not scattered,"
you ask, "so why did he need to walk about?" He did it
as an example so other living beings could imitate him
in their cultivation of the Way.

FOR A FULL THREE TIMES SEVEN DAYS/ For twenty-one
days I THOUGHT OVER MATTERS SUCH AS THESE/ What matters?
The matters concerned with teaching and transforming
living beings. THE WISDOM WHICH I HAVE OBTAINED/ IS
SUBTLE, WONDERFUL, AND FOREMOST/ BUT LIVING BEINGS ARE
DULL-ROOTED/ My wisdom is superb, but the dispositions
of living beings are exceedingly dull. They are quite
stupid. ATTACHED TO PLEASURE, BLINDED BY DELUSION/ They
are attached to and seduced by the happiness before
their eyes and are blinded by their own stupidity.
BEINGS SUCH AS THESE/ whose stupidity covers them
completely, HOW CAN THEY POSSIBLY BE SAVED/ They are
stupid because they have no wisdom. Their inherent
wisdom has been smothered by their delusion and desire.
Beings like this are as if blind. What can be done to
save these stupid living beings, to make them understand? Just as he was thinking about these things...

JUST THEN THE BRAHMA HEAVEN KINGS/ the kings in
the Brahma Heavens, AS WELL AS THE GOD SHAKRA/ Heavenly

Lord in the Heaven of the Thirty-three, THE FOUR WORLD-
PROTECTING GOD KINGS/ AS WELL AS THE GOD OF GREAT COM-
FORT/ As well as the ruler of the Maheshvara Heaven,
AND THE OTHER HEAVENLY MULTITUDES/ all the other gods
WITH RETINUES NUMBERING IN THE BILLIONS/ Every heavenly
king brought along a billion retainers and they REVER-
ENTLY PLACED THEIR PALMS TOGETHER/ AND REQUESTED ME TO
TURN THE DHARMA WHEEL/ The gods made obeisance to the
Buddha because they wanted him to teach the wonderful
Dharma.

I THEN THOUGHT TO MYSELF/ Since all the heavenly
hosts had asked me to speak the Dharma, I thought it
over once again. "WERE I TO PRAISE ONLY THE BUDDHA
VEHICLE/ and not mention the other Three Vehicles,
BEINGS SUNK IN SUFFERING/ Living beings would think,
"The Buddhadharma is so lofty and difficult. It takes
three great asankhyeya aeons to become a Buddha. I could
never do that." They would "gaze at the great sea and
heave a sigh." They wouldn't want to study the Dharma.
"There's no way I could ever learn something as great
and profound as the Buddhadharma," they would think.

Those who have never heard the Sutras take one
look at *The Dharma Flower Sutra* and think, "It's so big!
Two thick volumes. When will we ever finish listening
to it? Do I really have that much time?" And so they
don't listen. But once you have got a bit of the flavor
of the Buddhadharma, you will feel that the Dharma is
the most important thing in your life. It will stand in
the highest position. You will think, "Even if I don't
have time to eat, wear clothes, or sleep, I will certainly study the Buddhadharma." And whenever Sutras are
being lectured you will go to listen. According to the
rules in Buddhism, the lay people must go to Dharma
assemblies being conducted within forty miles of their
residence.

Living beings are sunk in suffering. They WOULD BE
UNABLE TO BELIEVE THIS DHARMA/ Because living beings are
so stupid, they would not believe you when you speak of
the Buddha Vehicle. THEY WOULD SLANDER IT OUT OF DIS-
BELIEF/ Their not believing themselves is not important,
but then they would try to ruin the Dharma. They would
slander the Dharma out of disbelief and thereby create
limitless, boundless offenses. AND FALL INTO THE THREE
EVIL PATHS/ One who slanders the wonderful Dharma of
the Real Teaching creates unbounded offenses and ends
up falling into the hells, into the animal realm, or
into the realm of hungry ghosts. They will end up like
the mother of the Brahman woman in *The Earth Store Bodhi-*

sattva Sutra. They will fall into the great hells.
Luckily, the Brahman woman's mother was a former incarnation of Earth Store Bodhisattva and the daughter
was able to rescue her mother and gain rebirth for her
in the heavens. We should each ask ourselves, can we
be sure that our son or daughter is Earth Store Bodhisattva or someone like him? After we have died, will
they come and rescue us? There's no guarantee, and so
we should bring forth a heart of genuine faith in the
Buddhadharma.

IT'S BETTER THAT I DO NOT SPEAK THE DHARMA/ The
Buddha thought to himself, "Because living beings
might slander the Dharma and fall into the three evil
paths, it would be better not to speak *The Wonderful
Dharma Lotus Flower Sutra*. BUT QUICKLY ENTER INTO NIRVANA/
I will go to Nirvana. I will not remain in the world
to turn the Dharma Wheel.

Sutra: (T.262, 9c17)

52-154 Then I recalled that the Buddhas of the past

Practiced powerful expedients,

And as I now have obtained the Path,

It's fitting that I also teach Three Vehicles.

When I had been thinking thus,

5-156 The Buddhas of the ten directions all appeared,

And with the Brahma sound encouraged me, saying,

"Good indeed, O Shakyamuni,

Foremost Guiding Master.

Having attained the supreme Dharma,

You follow the precedent of all Buddhas,

To employ the power of expedient devices.

We have all obtained as well,

That foremost Dharma, most wonderful.

For the various kinds of living beings,

We discriminate and teach Three Vehicles.

Those of little wisdom who delight in lesser dharmas,

Would not believe that they could become Buddhas.

That is why we use expedient means,

To discriminate and teach the various fruits.

Although Three Vehicles are taught,

It is only for the sake of teaching Bodhisattvas.

Commentary:

THEN I RECALLED THAT THE BUDDHAS OF THE PAST/ After a bit it occurred to me that all the Buddhas of the past had PRACTICED POWERFUL EXPEDIENTS/ AND AS I NOW HAVE OBTAINED THE PATH/ IT IS FITTING THAT I SPEAK THREE VEHICLES/ I should also bestow the provisional teaching for the sake of the real teaching and speak of the doctrine of the Three Vehicles. WHEN I HAD BEEN THINK-ING THUS/ THE BUDDHAS OF THE TEN DIRECTIONS ALL APPEAR-ED/ AND WITH THE BRAHMA SOUND ENCOURAGED ME, SAYING/ They used the clear, pure Buddha-sound to encourage me. They chatted with me, saying, GOOD INDEED, O SHAKYA-MUNI/ Very fine, very fine, Shakyamuni, FOREMOST GUIDING MASTER/ You are really the number one teacher in the world. HAVING ATTAINED THE SUPREME DHARMA/ You have obtained the supreme and wonderful Dharma, and what is more YOU FOLLOW THE PRECEDENT OF ALL BUDDHAS/ TO EMPLOY THE POWER OF EXPEDIENT DEVICES/ You follow the example of the Buddhas of the ten directions in using provisional, expedient devices.

WE HAVE ALL OBTAINED AS WELL/ THAT FOREMOST DHARMA MOST WONDERFUL/ FOR THE VARIOUS KINDS OF LIVING BEINGS/ however, WE DISCRIMINATE AND TEACH THREE VEHICLES/ Be-cause living beings differ in their potential to re-ceive the teachings, we establish various provisional devices, teaching the Sound Hearer Vehicle, the Con-ditioned Enlightened Vehicle, and the Bodhisattva Vehicle.

THOSE OF LITTLE WISDOM WHO DELIGHT IN LESSER DHARMAS/ Stupid people have very little wisdom, and so they like the lesser dharmas. They don't have the disposition for the great Dharma. They are like child-ren who can only play with small toys. If you give them something too big, they can't play with it. You can only teach the small vehicle Dharma to small vehicle people. If you try to teach them the Great Vehicle, they just get all confused. They don't understand it. WOULD NOT BELIEVE THAT THEY COULD BECOME BUDDHAS/ Why do they delight in the lesser dharmas and fail to under-stand the great Dharma? It's because they don't believe that they can become Buddhas. THAT IS WHY WE USE EX-PEDIENT MEANS/ provisional Dharma-doors, TO DISCRIMIN-ATE AND TEACH THE VARIOUS FRUITS/ speaking of the first,

second, third, and fourth fruits of Arhatship. ALTHOUGH
THREE VEHICLES ARE TAUGHT/ IT IS ONLY FOR THE SAKE OF
TEACHING BODHISATTVAS/ In actuality, the Three Vehicles
are only taught to teach and transform Bodhisattvas, to
lead them to cultivate the Dharma-door of the One
Buddha Vehicle.

Sutra: (T.262, 9c28)

157

> Shariputra, you should know,
>
> That when I heard the Sagely Lions'
>
> Deep, pure, and wondrous sound,
>
> I called out "Homage to all Buddhas."
>
> And further had this thought,
>
> "I have come into a turbid, evil world;
>
> As the Buddhas speak,
>
> I should follow in accord."

158

> Having thought upon this matter,
>
> I went straightway to Varanasi.
>
> Since the still and extinct mark of all dharmas,
>
> Cannot be expressed in words,
>
> I used the power of expedients,
>
> To instruct the five Bhikshus.

Commentary:

SHARIPUTRA, YOU SHOULD KNOW/ THAT WHEN I HEARD
THE SAGELY LIONS'/ when I heard the Buddhas of the ten
directions praising me in this way, saying that I was
number one, great guiding master, DEEP, PURE, AND WON-
DROUS SOUND/ Their sound was clear and fine, so I
CALLED OUT "HOMAGE TO ALL BUDDHAS"/ The Buddhas having
praised Shakyamuni Buddha, Shakyamuni Buddha then
praised them. This is the Buddhas praising each other.
AND FURTHER HAD THIS THOUGHT/ "I HAVE COME INTO A
TURBID, EVIL WORLD/ I have now appeared in the Saha
world, a world of five turbidities, an evil world.
AS THE BUDDHAS SPEAK/ I SHOULD FOLLOW IN ACCORD/ Since
I have come into this evil world, I should speak the
Dharma in the same manner as all the Buddhas of the
ten directions. I should employ the same methods.
HAVING THOUGHT UPON THIS MATTER/ When I was done
thinking this thing over, I WENT STRAIGHTWAY TO

VARANASI/ Varanasi is the Deer Park. Why do they call
it the "Deer Park?"
    Once, there were two deer kings living there. One
deer king was a former incarnation, many births and
many aeons ago, of Shakyamuni Buddha. He was the
compassionate deer king. The other deer king was a
former incarnation of Devadatta. At that time, the king
of the country often went out to hunt deer. He took
many people along with him, and killed many deer on
every expedition. So many deer were killed that they
were on the verge of becoming extinct altogether.
The two deer kings had a meeting and decided that the
deer king who was to become a Buddha would go present
a petition to the king, begging him for clemency.
    "What kind of petition shall we present?" asked
the other deer king.
    The compassionate deer king said, "We shall tell
the king that everyday we will send him two deer for
his food. Then our herds will not become extinct
and the king will have fresh venison everyday. I'm
sure the king will agree to this. If he doesn't,
pretty soon we will all be dead and he won't have
any deer meat at all. Besides, he can't possibly eat
that much meat. I'll bet he lets most of it rot."
    The deer king Devadatta said, "Okay, let's go
ask him!" and the two of them went to the palace to
present their request. When they arrived at the gate,
they met the palace guard, who immediately drew his
sword to slaughter them.
    "Don't kill us!" the two deer cried. "We have
come today for an audience with the king. We want to
present him with a petition.
    The guard was quite taken aback. "Weird," he
said, "talking deer!" and he ran to tell the king
that two *talking* deer, for heaven's sake, had come to
see the king.
    The king raised an eyebrow and looked at the
guard, "Talking deer? Oh yes, well tell them to come
in and we will see what kind of strange creatures
they are."
    The two deer came in and politely spoke with the
king. "You've been hunting our herds, Your Majesty,
and many of our deer have been killed. You can't
possibly eat that much meat everyday, can you? If
you keep it up we will disappear altogether and you
won't have any meat to eat. So we have a petition
to present to you. Everyday we will send two deer
for you to eat. Then you won't have to go hunting
but you will have meat to eat everyday." At that time

there were no refrigerators. "If you continue to kill us at the rate you have been, you'll wipe us out."

The king was already surprised to hear deer talking like people. He thought their request was logically very sound and agreed. "Everyday you can send us two deer," he said. And that's just what they did.

One day, the deer king who was to become Shakyamuni Buddha appeared at the palace gate as food for the king. The king recognized the deer and said, "You're the king of the deer. How can you offer yourself? Have all the other deer in your herd been eaten or what?

The compassioante deer king said, "Not only do there remain deer in our herds, but their numbers are increasing daily. We two deer kings each watch over five hundred deer. Of the five hundred, only one goes each day as an offering to Your Majesty. Everyday many fawns are born. So now, our retinues have redoubled several times over. But now, for a special reason, I myself have come as your daily offering."

"But why?" asked the king.

"Today's deer from my herd came with no problems, but in Devadatta's herd there was trouble. The deer selected to go happened to be pregnant. Her baby was due in a day or two and she begged Devadatta to let her trade places with someone else, saying that when her baby was born she would gladly go to the king for food. But Devadatta wouldn't hear of it. She came to me and asked me if a deer in my herd would trade with her. None of my deer wanted to go, of course, so I volunteered myself and here I am."

When the king heard this he thought, "How strange. Basically, deer are living creatures, just like people. Why should I eat deer meat everyday? They have feelings just like people do." Then he chanted a verse:

> "You are a person with a deer's head," he cried.
> And though I am a person
> I'm just a deer inside.
> But from this day forward
> only vegetables I'll eat;
> I will never ever eat
> another living being's meat."

"You have the head of a deer," he said, "but your heart is extremely kind and compassionate. Your heart is even bigger than that of most human beings. Now, I may have a person's head, but my heart is not as good as that of a deer. From today on, I am not going to eat meat." And so the king was moved to become a vege-

tarian. This is the reason that this particular place
was called the Deer Park. It was a place of blue
mountains and crystal streams. There were many cultivators there.

In the past, Shakyamuni Buddha had five fellow
cultivators. Three were relatives on his father's
side and two were relatives on his mother's side. They
followed him when he left home and cultivated with him.
However, three of them couldn't endure the suffering
and ran away. Shakyamuni Buddha, while meditating in
the Himalayas, ate only one sesame seed and one grain
of rice a day. Three of them couldn't take it, and
ran off to the Deer Park. Two remained with the Buddha.
At that time, the Buddha was so thin that he looked
like a heap of firewood. Then a shepherdess brought
him an offering of rice gruel and milk. The Buddha
was very pleased, and ate it. His two companions
exclaimed, "He's finished! He's useless! He'll never
realize the Way. What a glutton! Someone gives him
some milk and he drinks it! Cultivating means enduring
suffering, and he can no longer endure it, obviously.
We're not going to stick around with someone like
that. Let's go!" So the Buddha was left all by himself.

Later, he went to sit beneath the Bodhi tree.
One night, he saw a bright star and awoke to the Way.

Shakymuni Buddha endured a great deal of bitterness in his cultivation. And we run into a bit of
difficulty and can't stand it. How do we measure up to
Shakyamuni Buddha?

SINCE THE STILL AND EXTINCT MARK OF DHARMAS/
CANNOT BE EXPRESSED IN WORDS/ When the Buddha went to
the Deer Park to teach, he knew that all dharmas are
marked with still extinction; they have no appearance.
The mark of still extinction, however, is basically
ineffable, that is, you can't express it in words.

> The path of language has come to an end,
> The place of the mind's activity
> has been cast out.

I USED THE POWER OF EXPEDIENTS/ TO INSTRUCT THE
FIVE BHIKSHUS/ He spoke the Dharma for the sake of
Ajnata-kaundinya and the others. The five Bhikshus were
the first to receive the Buddha's teaching when he went
to the Deer Park after realizing the Way. They were the
five who had accompanied him when he left home. Three of
them ran off because they were afraid of suffering and
two of them ran off because they were afraid of enjoying themselves. Then, after the Buddha realized the
Way, he observed the causes and conditions and saw the
five Bhikshus cultivating in the Deer Park. He decided

that he should first go to the Deer Park and teach the
five Bhikshus the three turnings of the Four Truths.

Sutra: (T.262 10a6)

159 This was called the turning of the Dharma wheel.

Then came the sound of Nirvana,

As well as "Arhatship,"

"Dharma," and the "Sangha," various names.

160 From remote aeons onward,

I have praised and shown Nirvana's dharma,

As the final end of birth and death's sufferings;

Always have I spoken thus.

161 Shariputra, you should know,

I see disciples of the Buddha,

Resolutely seeking the Buddha Way,

Limitless thousands of myriads of millions of them,

All with hearts of reverence,

All coming before the Buddha.

They had heard, from former Buddhas,

Expedient teachings of the Dharma.

This causes me to think,

"The reason why the Thus Come One appears,

Is to teach the wisdom of the Buddha,

And now the time is exactly right."

Shariputra, you should know,

Those with dull faculties and slight wisdom,

Those attached to marks, the arrogant,

Cannot believe this Dharma.

I now rejoice and have no fear,

And among the Bodhisattvas,

I shall cast expedients aside,

To speak only of the supreme Path.

When the Bodhisattvas have heard this Dharma,

The network of their doubts will be rent;

Twelve hundred Arhats
Will all attain to Buddhahood.

Commentary:

THIS WAS CALLED THE TURNING OF THE DHARMA WHEEL/
What is meant by "the three turnings of the Four
Truths?"

The Buddha expounded upon the Four Truths in three
ways, called "three turnings." In the first turning
he said to the five Bhikshus:
1. This is suffering; its nature is oppressive.
2. This is origination; it's nature is
seductive.
3. This is extinction; its nature is that it can
be certified to.
4. This is the Way; its nature is that it can be
cultivated.
He said, "This is suffering. It is oppressive.
This is origination. It has the nature of seduction.
It comes through craving. You bring this affliction
upon yourself. This is extinction. Extinction refers
to the still extinction of Nirvana with its four
virtues of permanence, bliss, true self, and purity.
You can certify to extinction. This is the Way. You
can cultivate it, and thereby certify to the four
virtues of Nirvana.
In the second turning, he said,
1. This is suffering; I already know it.
2. This is origination; I have already severed it.
3. This is extinction; I have already
certified to it.
4. This is the Way; I have already cultivated it.
I already know about suffering. I have already
cut off afflictions. As to extinction, the four virtues
of Nirvana, I have already certified to the attainment
of that doctrine. As to the Way, I have already cultivated it with success. I have cultivated the Thirty-
seven Wings of enlightenment.
In the third turning, he said,
1. This is suffering; you should know it.
2. This is origination; you should cut it off.
3. This is extinction; you should certify to it.
4. This is the Way; you should cultivate it.
This is suffering and you also should understand
it. This is origination. This affliction is the "guest
dust." It is not the host. It comes from outside and
so it has the "nature of seduction. In *The Shurangama*

Sutra we read about the "guest dust." It was because
of the two words "guest dust" that Ajnatakaundinya
became enlightened. "A guest," he said, "doesn't stay
forever. In the future it's going to leave." He became
enlightened because of the two words "guest dust" and
his name means, "the first to be released." or "understanding the original limit." As to extinction, you
should certify to it, too. And you should also cultivate the Way.

When the Buddha said these things to the five
Bhikshus, Ajnatakaundinya understood and certified to
the fruit. That was called the three turnings of the
Four Holy Truths.

THEN CAME THE SOUND OF NIRVANA/ Because he had
turned the Dharma Wheel of the Four Truths, he had
spoken of still, extinct Nirvana. AS WELL AS "ARHATSHIP"/
The term "Arhat" also came into use. There were first,
second, third, and fourth stage Arhats. "DHARMA," AND
THE "SANGHA," VARIOUS NAMES/ The Dharma refers to the
Dharma of the Four Truths. The Sangha refers to the
Arhats.

FROM REMOTE AEONS ONWARDS/ From the distant past,
while cultivating the Dharma I HAVE PRAISED AND SHOWN
NIRVANA'S DHARMA/ I have lauded the dharma of Nirvana.
AS THE FINAL END OF BIRTH AND DEATH'S SUFFERINGS/ If you
can certify to the happiness of Nirvana, to that wonderful doctrine, then you will have severed for all time
the sufferings of birth and death. They will be gone
forever. ALWAYS HAVE I SPOKEN THUS/ I have told you
this over and over, constantly. From distant aeons onward in every life I have spoken this dharma for you.

SHARIPUTRA, YOU SHOULD KNOW/ You ought to know
I SEE DISCIPLES OF THE BUDDHA/ RESOLUTELY SEEKING THE
BUDDHA WAY/ LIMITLESS THOUSANDS OF MYRIADS OF MILLIONS
OF THEM/ ALL WITH HEARTS OF REVERENCE/ ALL COMING BE-
FORE THE BUDDHA/ They all came to see the Buddha.
THEY HAD HEARD, FROM FORMER BUDDHAS/ In past lives, they
had heard the Dharma from the Buddhas. EXPEDIENT TEACH-
INGS OF THE DHARMA/ THIS CAUSES ME TO THINK/ Just now,
it occurs to me THE REASON THE THUS COME ONE APPEARS/
in the world IS TO TEACH THE WISDOM OF THE BUDDHA/ to
teach the genuine, real Buddha-wisdom. AND NOW THE TIME
IS EXACTLY RIGHT/ SHARIPUTRA, YOU SHOULD KNOW/ THOSE
WITH DULL-FACULTIES AND SLIGHT WISDOM/ Stupid, dim-
witted people with precious little wisdom, THOSE ATTACH-
ED TO MARKS, THE ARROGANT/ They are attached to marks,
they are attached to everything, and what is more, they
are arrogant and think that they are terribly important.

CANNOT BELIEVE THIS DHARMA/ They won't be able to hear
The Wonderful Dharma Lotus Flower Sutra. And, in fact, five
thousand people did walk out.

I NOW REJOICE AND HAVE NO FEAR/ All of those without good roots, all of the arrogant ones have left.
I am now happy and fearless. I'm not worried at all.
AND AMONG THE BODHISATTVAS/ I SHALL CAST EXPEDIENTS
ASIDE/ I will not use expedient means. I will now
open the gate, so you can see the mountain. I will
frankly and straightforwardly explain the genuine
wisdom. I'm getting rid of the expedients. I'll use
them no more. I will only speak the Dharma-door of
realizing Buddhahood.

WHEN THE BODHISATTVAS HAVE HEARD THIS DHARMA/
The Wonderful Dharma Lotus Flower Sutra, THE NETWORK OF THEIR
DOUBTS WILL BE RENT/ All their doubts will vanish.

TWELVE HUNDRED ARHATS/ WILL ALL ATTAIN TO BUDDHA-
HOOD/ In the future they will all become Buddhas. Here
the Buddha gives all of his disciples predictions of
future Buddhahood. So, in the Dharma Flower Assembly there
is not one who will not become a Budana. Those who have
attended the Dharma Flower Assembly will all become
Buddhas.

The wonderful Dharma is hard to meet. What is more,
it is hard to hear it. In a hundred million aeons, it
is not easy to encounter *The Wonderful Dharma Lotus Flower
Sutra.* Though one encounters it, it is even more difficult to be able to read and recite it. If you are
able to read and recite it, then to understand the
doctrines contained within it is hard to do in a
million aeons. Having encountered it, it is difficult
to hear it explained. Now, in the entire world, there
are very few places where one can hear this Sutra. Rare
as it is, we are now explaning it. In the future, we
will hear *The Great Avatamsaka Sutra,* which is even more
difficult to encounter. In China during the past hundred
years, it would be hard to find one occasion when *The
Avatamsaka Sutra* was lectured.

The doctrines in *The Wonderful Dharma Lotus Flower
Sutra* are ineffably wonderful. But the doctrines in
The Great Avatamsaka Sutra are even more wonderful. In order
to explain *The Avatamsaka Sutra,* one must have a solid
foundation in learning. Otherwise, one wouldn't be able
to understand much less explain, it. One passage says
that those who cultivate Dhyana samadhi will emerge
from proper samadhi in the east and enter samadhi in
the west. They will enter proper samadhi in the south
and emerge from it in the north. It says they will
enter samadhi through the nose, and emerge from sam-

adhi through the tongue. What does that mean? What
does it mean to enter proper samadhi from the nose
and come out through the tongue? Within the six organs,
you enter through one and emerge through another. Who's
coming and who's leaving?

So, in the future, if there are those who like to
study the Buddhadharma, and who wish to understand it,
the opportunity will present itself. In the future,
if you want to seek the Dharma you won't have to go all
the way to India like China's Hsüan Tsang did. He ran
off to India to seek the Dharma and ran until his feet
broke open. He wore himself out. Now, you can sit in
your very own country and hear such wonderful Dharma.
In the future, your opportunities will be even finer
than those of Dharma Master Hsüan Tsang.

Sutra: (T.262 10a22)

162 As the Buddhas of the three periods of time

In such a manner spoke the Dharma,

So do I likewise now expound

The undiscriminated Dharma.

All Buddhas come into the world

But rarely, and are hard to meet;

And when they appear in the world,

It's hard for them to speak the Dharma.

Throughout countless ages, too,

It's difficult to hear this Dharma.

And those who can hear this Dharma--

Such people   too, are rare,

Like the udumbara flower,

In which all take delight,

Which the gods and humans prize,

For it blooms but once in a long, long time.

So one who hears this Dharma, gives joyful praise,

With even just a single word,

Has thereby made offerings,

To all the Buddhas of the three periods of time.

Such people are extremely rare,

Rarer than the udumbara flower.

Commentary:

AS THE BUDDHAS OF THE THREE PERIODS OF TIME/ IN
SUCH A MANNER SPOKE THE DHARMA/ Shakyamuni Buddha says,
"I now speak the real Buddhadharma, the teaching of
real wisdom, the Buddha Vehicle. I do so in the same
manner as did all the Buddhas of the past, present,
and future. SO DO I LIKEWISE EXPOUND/ THE UNDISCRIMIN-
ATED DHARMA/ I speak the most subtle and wonderful
Dharma of the One Buddha Vehicle, the only Vehicle.
There are no other vehicles. That is the undiscrimin-
ated Dharma which cannot be understood with one's
ordinary conscious mind.
ALL BUDDHAS COME INTO THE WORLD/ BUT RARELY AND
ARE HARD TO MEET/ To be able to meet with a Buddha
is very rare. It happens but once in a long while.
AND WHEN THEY APPEAR IN THE WORLD/ IT'S HARD FOR THEM
TO SPEAK THIS DHARMA/ Even if you should meet with
a Buddha appearing in the world, it is extremely rare
for the Buddha to speak *The Wonderful Dharma Lotus Flower
Sutra.* The Buddha taught the Storehouse Teaching,
then the Agamas, and then the Vaipulya and Prajna
Teachings. It was not until the very end that he spoke
The Dharma Flower Sutra.
THROUGHOUT COUNTLESS AGES, TOO/ IT'S DIFFICULT
TO HEAR THIS DHARMA/ To be able to hear this Dharma
is also difficult. Our present Dharma Flower Assembly
is most rare.
AND THOSE WHO CAN HEAR THIS DHARMA/ SUCH PEOPLE,
TOO, ARE RARE/ LIKE THE UDUMBARA FLOWER/ which blooms
only once every three thousand years. Once it blooms,
it quickly fades. IN WHICH ALL TAKE DELIGHT/ WHICH THE
GODS AND HUMANS PRIZE/ FOR IT BLOOMS BUT ONCE IN A
LONG, LONG TIME/ All prize it because it is so rare.
It will not bloom until the time is right.
SO ONE WHO HEARS THIS DHARMA, AND GIVES JOYFUL PRAISE/
WITH EVEN JUST A SINGLE WORD/ HAS THEREBY MADE OFFER-
INGS/ TO ALL THE BUDDHAS OF THE THREE PERIODS OF TIME/
One who hears *The Wonderful Dharma Lotus Flower Sutra* and
who praises it with even just a single word, saying,
"This Sutra is really wonderful," has made offerings
to all the Buddhas. SUCH PEOPLE ARE EXTREMELY RARE/
RARER THAN THE UDUMBARA/ The udumbara flower blooms
once every three thousand years, but this person is
even rarer. So you can see that it is difficult to hear
the Dharma. Such causal affinities are hard to come by.

This means that we should be very happy to hear it now.
Throughout limitless ages, we have planted vast good
roots, and today the good roots have ripened, enabling
us to hear the Sutra. Without good roots, you would
never have had the chance to hear it.

Sutra: (T.262 10b4)

163 All of you should have no doubts,

    For I am the Dharma King;

    I declare to the assembly:

    I use only the path of One Vehicle,

    To teach and transform Bodhisattvas.

    There are no Sound Hearer Disciples.

    Shariputra, all of you,

    the Sound Hearers and Bodhisattvas,

    Should know that this wondrous Dharma

    Is the secret essence of all Buddhas.

Commentary:

ALL OF YOU SHOULD HAVE NO DOUBTS/ Shakyamuni Buddha
says, "Take care, all of you, not to doubt this Dharma
I have spoken. Why? FOR I AM THE DHARMA KING/ I am the
king of all dharmas, having obtained the real, true
wisdom. I DECLARE TO THE ASSEMBLY/ I will now use my
trustworthy, true words to tell all of you in the
Dharma gathering as well as those assemblies of the
future, that I USE ONLY THE PATH OF ONE VEHICLE/ I use
only the path of the One Buddha Vehicle, the Vehicle
of realizing Buddhahood TO TEACH AND TRANSFORM BODHI-
SATTVAS/ THERE ARE NO SOUND HEARER DISCIPLES/ There
is no Small Vehicle dharma.

SHARIPUTRA, ALL OF YOU/ THE SOUND HEARERS AND
BODHISATTVAS/ SHOULD KNOW THAT THIS WONDROUS DHARMA/
this Dharma of the Great Vehicle, IS THE SECRET
ESSENCE OF ALL BUDDHAS/ You should return from the
small and head towards the great. Don't continue to
be satisfied with obtaining just a little. Don't draw
the line for yourself in the middle of the road saying,
"This is it; I'm stopping here. I don't want to go any
further." You should know that this wonderful Dharma
spoken by all the Buddhas in *The Wonderful Dharma Lotus
Flower Sutra,* is the most esoteric, most important, and
most wonderful Dharma. It is spoken by all the Buddhas

in the ten directions and the three periods of time.
Whatever you do, don't doubt it.

Sutra: (T.262 10b9)

164-165 In the evil world of five turbidities,

  Beings who are blissfully attached

  To pleasures and desires,

  Will never seek the Buddha Way.

  Evil people of the future,

  Hearing the Buddha speak of One Vehicle,

  In their delusion will not accept or believe it,

  But will slander it and fall into the evil paths.

  Still, those with shame and purity,

  Who resolutely seek the Buddha Way,

  For such ones as these I praise

  The path of One Vehicle, extensively.

Commentary:

  IN THE EVIL WORLD OF FIVE TURBIDITIES/ the aeon
turbidity, the view turbidity, the affliction turbidity,
the living beings turbidity, and the life turbidity,
BEINGS WHO ARE BLISSFULLY ATTACHED/ TO PLEASURES AND
DESIRES/ who crave sensual pleasures, and are greedy
for the objects of their desires, WILL NEVER SEEK THE
BUDDHA WAY/ They are greedy for temporary happiness.
Everyone is confused by these temproary pleasures. They
are confused because they don't understand them. For
example, people have various desires. Those greedy for
wealth are confused by wealth. Those greedy for forms
are confused by beauty. Those greedy for food are confused by food and drink. Those greedy for drugs are
confused by drugs. They take some drugs and think,
"Probably I didn't take enough and that's why I didn't
get enlightened. There's some hope if I take a larger
dose next time." This is pathetic. It is totally impossible, but they try it anyway. The more confused
they are, the more confused they get. Their confusion
grows deeper and deeper. The deeper their confusion,
the stronger their craving. Whatever you desire, you are
confused by that desire. If you are confused by it, you
cannot free yourself. You are caught in your desire as
if you were caught in quicksand. You get one leg out,

but the other is still caught. Then you get the other
leg out and the first leg gets stuck again. The Buddha
knew long ago that there would be such deluded people.
It will never occur to them to seek the Buddha Way, to
bring forth genuine wisdom, or to break through their
confusion.

The *Wonderful Dharma Lotus Flower Sutra* is the secret
essence of all the Buddhas. Shakyamuni Buddha waited a
long time to speak it. He waited because it was too
important. If this Dharma were spoken, living beings
would not believe it. They would slander it and fall
into the three evil paths.

EVIL PEOPLE OF THE FUTURE/ That's just right now.
The Buddha knew long ago that there would be evil
people who HEARING THE BUDDHA SPEAK OF ONE VEHICLE/
IN THEIR DELUSION WILL NOT ACCEPT OR BELIEVE IT/ They
will doubt *The Dharma Flower Sutra*. They will wonder, "What's
he talking about? What does he mean 'become a Buddha?'"
BUT WILL SLANDER IT AND FALL INTO THE EVIL PATHS/ Not
only will they refuse to believe it, but they will
slander it. They will say, "He says that's the Buddhadharma, but there's no such thing." In this way they
will fall into the hells, into the realm of the animals
or hungry ghosts.

STILL, THOSE WITH SHAME AND PURITY/ Those who
know enough to be ashamed of their mistakes and who
resolve to reform themselves in the future, those who
are pure in their cultivation, WHO RESOLUTELY SEEK THE
BUDDHA WAY/ who are determined to become Buddhas, FOR
SUCH ONES AS THESE I PRAISE/ THE PATH OF ONE VEHICLE,
EXTENSIVELY/ I speak *The Wonderful Dharma Lotus Flower Sutra*,
praising the Buddha Way of One Vehicle.

Sutra: (T.262 10b15)

166
Shariputra, you should know,

The Dharma of all Buddhas is like this:

By means of millions of expedients,

I speak Dharma in accord with what's appropriate.

But those who do not study it,

Will never come to understand it.

Since all of you already know

All Buddhas, Masters of the World,

Work by means of appropriate expedients,

You should have no further doubts.

Let your hearts be filled with joy;

You know you will reach Buddhahood.

Commentary:

SHARIPUTRA, YOU SHOULD KNOW/ You and all the
Bhikshus, Bhikshunis, Upasakas, Upasikas, the gods,
dragons, and the rest of the eight-fold division--
you should all be informed that THE DHARMA OF ALL BUDDHAS
IS LIKE THIS/ The Buddhas of the ten directions all have
the same identical path. All the Buddhas are the same.
So it is said,

> All Buddhas of the three periods of time
> and the ten directions,
> Have the same identical Dharma body.

Their Dharma body is one and their Dharma is
"Thus." The Dharma of all Buddhas is the same. It is
like the wonderful Dharma of *The Wonderful Dharma Lotus
Flower Sutra*. The Buddhas observe the potentials of
living beings and BY MEANS OF MILLIONS OF EXPEDIENTS/
I SPEAK DHARMA IN ACCORD WITH WHAT'S APPROPRIATE/
using millions of different methods to teach and transform living beings. When living beings need a particular
dharma, the Buddha teaches it to them.

BUT THOSE WHO DO NOT STUDY IT/ WILL NEVER COME TO
UNDERSTAND IT/ Although the Buddha speaks the Dharma
for them, if they do not study it and put it into
practice, they will never be able to understand it.
You must study and practice it before you can understand it. Since they do not understand the Buddhadharma,
they will not, of course, be able to cultivate according
to it. Unable to cultivate according to it, they will
not be able to become Buddhas.

SINCE ALL OF YOU ALREADY KNOW/ ALL BUDDHAS, MASTERS
OF THE WORLD/ Shariputra, you and all the great Arhats,
great Bodhisattvas, great Bhikshus and others, already
know the genuine, wonderful Dharma is set forth by the
Buddhas, the Masters of the World. They WORK BY MEANS
OF APPROPRIATE EXPEDIENTS/ The Buddhas use clever,
expedient devices to teach living beings. Since you
know this YOU SHOULD HAVE NO FURTHER DOUBTS/ LET YOUR
HEARTS BE FILLED WITH JOY/ Hearing *The Wonderful Dharma
Lotus Flower Sutra,* you should be very happy. You should
remember that it is difficult to encounter. Such
affinities are not easy to come by.

YOU KNOW YOU WILL REACH BUDDHAHOOD/ Each one of
you should know that you will certainly realize Buddha-

hood. So, in the Dharma Flower Assembly, all living beings are assured of their future Buddhahood. Shakyamuni Buddha has given them all predictions to that effect.

This concludes the second chapter and the first roll of *The Dharma Flower Sutra*. I will now explain the verse in praise that follows the end of this roll:

> The world Honored One manifests portents;
> Maitreya wondered about the auspicious signs.
> Manjushri explained them extensively
>   for the sake of those assembled.
> The ancient Buddhas emitted the white hair light;
> The Dharma was requested thrice,
> To set forth the fragrance of the wonderful lotus.
>
> Homage to the Dharma Flower Assembly of
> Buddhas and Bodhisattvas (3x).

This verse sums up the first two chapters of the Sutra. THE WORLD HONORED ONE MANIFESTS PORTENTS/ The Buddha manifested six portents and so MAITREYA WONDERED ABOUT THE AUSPICIOUS SIGNS/ Maitreya Bodhisattva didn't understand why the Buddha manifested the portents. MANJUSHRI EXPLAINED THEM EXTENSIVELY FOR THE SAKE OF THOSE ASSEMBLED/ THE ANCIENT BUDDHAS EMITTED THE WHITE HAIR LIGHT/ THE DHARMA WAS REQUESTED THRICE/ Shariputra requested the Buddha to speak the Dharma three times. TO SET FORTH THE FRAGRANCE OF THE WONDERFUL LOTUS/ to speak *The Wonderful Dharma Lotus Flower Sutra*.

HOMAGE TO THE DHARMA FLOWER ASSEMBLY OF BUDDHAS AND BODHISATTVAS/ In just reciting this phrase, you gain unlimited merit and virtue. So in Japan, people recite it over and over, thinking they will gain great benefit. If they don't have a job, they get one. If they don't have food, they get food. If they don't have tea to drink, they get tea to drink. If they don't have wine to drink, they get wine to drink. It's incredibly wonderful, so they think.

For now, however, I have food, so I don't need to recite it right now, just explain it.

END OF CHAPTER TWO, ROLL ONE--*THE DHARMA FLOWER SUTRA*

514

518

THE BUDDHIST TEXT TRANSLATION SOCIETY

Chairperson: The Venerable Master Hua, Abbot of Gold Mountain
Monastery, Professor of the Tripitaka
and the Dhyanas

PRIMARY TRANSLATION COMMITTEE:
Chairpersons: Bhikshuni Heng Yin, Lecturer in Buddhism
Bhikshuni Heng Ch'ih, Lecturer in Buddhism

Members: Bhikshu Wei Sung, Lecturer in Buddhism
Bhikshu Heng Kuan, Lecturer in Buddhism
Bhikshu Heng Sure, Lecturer in Buddhism
Bhikshuni Heng Hsien, Lecturer in Buddhism
Bhikshuni Heng Ch'ing, Lecturer in Buddhism
Shramanerika Kuo Ching
Upasaka Huang Kuo-jen, Kung-fu Master, B.A.
Upasaka I Kuo-jung, Ph.D., U.C. Berkeley

REVISION COMMITTEE:

Chairperson: Upasaka I Kuo-jung

Members: Bhikshu Heng Kuan
Bhikshu Heng Sure
Bhikshuni Heng Yin
Bhikshuni Heng Hsien
Professor Lewis Lancaster, U.C. Berkeley
Professor M. Tseng, San Francisco State University
Upasaka Hsieh Ping-ying, author, professor, editor
Upasika Phoung Kuo-wu
Upasaka Lee Kuo-ch'ien, B.A.
Upasaka Li Kuo-wi, M.A.
Upasika I Kuo-han, B.A.
Upasika Kuo-ts'an Epstein
Upasika Kuo-chin Vickers

EDITORIAL COMMITTEE:

Chairperson: Bhikshu Heng Kuan

Members: Bhikshu Heng Sure
Bhikshu Heng Shun
Bhikshuni Heng Yin
Bhikshuni Heng Ch'ih
Bhikshuni Heng hsien
Bhikshuni Heng Chü
Bhikshuni Heng Ch'ing
Professor Irving Lo, University of Indiana

Upasaka I Kuo-jung
Upasaka Kuo K'uei Bach
Upasaka Kuo Chou Rounds,B.A., Harvard
Upasika Kuo Chin Vickers
Upasika Kuo Tsong Bach
Upasaka Kuo T'ang Yager, Ph.D., Columbia
Upasika Kuo Chao Eberle
Upasika Kuo Ts'u Smith
Upasika Kuo Ling Berger
Upasaka Kuo Tsun Dinwiddie, B.A. University of Washington
Upasika Kuo Hsun Nolan, B.A., San Franciso State University

CERTIFICATION COMMITTEE:

Chairperson: The Venerable Master Hua

Members: Bhikshu Heng Kuan
               Bhikshuni Heng Yin
               Bhikshuni Heng Ch'ih
               Bhikshuni Heng Hsien

Upasaka Wong Kuo-chun
Upasaka I Kuo-jung
Upasika T'an Kuo-shih, B.A.
Upasika Kuo-chin Vickers

THE BUDDHIST TEXT TRANSLATION SOCIETY

The Buddhist Text Translation Society is dedicated to making the genuine principles of the Buddhadharma available to the Western reader in a form that can be put directly into practice. Since 1972, the Society has been publishing English translations of Sutras, instructional handbooks in meditation and moral conduct, biographies, poetry, and fiction. Each of the Society's translations is accompanied by a contemporary commentary spoken by the Venerable Master Hsüan Hua. The Venerable Master Hua is the founder of Gold Mountain Monastery and the Institute for the Translation of Buddhist Texts, both located in San Francisco, as well as Gold Wheel Temple in Los Angeles, and the new center of world Buddhism, the City of Ten Thousand Buddhas, near Ukiah, California.

The accurate and faithful translation of the Buddhist Canon into English and other Western languages is one of the most important objectives of the Sino-American Buddhist Association, the parent organization of the Buddhist Text Translation Society.

EIGHT REGULATIONS FOR TRANSLATION SOCIETY TRANSLATORS:

The translation of the Buddhist Tripitaka is a work of such magnitude that it could never be entrusted to a single person working on his own. Above all, translations of Sutras must be certified as the authentic transmission of the Buddha's proper Dharma. Translations done under the auspices of the Buddhist Text Translation Society, a body of more than thirty Sangha members and scholars, bear such authority. The following eight regulations govern the conduct of   Text Translation Society Translators:

1. A translator must free himself from motives of personal gain and reputation.
2. A translator must cultivate an attitude free from arrogance and conceit.
3. A translator must refrain from advertising himself and denigrating others.
4. A translator must not establish himself as the standard of correctness and supress the work of others with his fault-finding.
5. A translator must take the Buddha-mind as his own mind.
6. A translator must use the wisdom of the selective Dharma-eye to determine true principles.
7. A translator must request the Virtuous Elders from the ten directions to certify his translations.
8. A translator must endeavor to propagate the teachings by printing Sutras, Shastras, and Vinaya texts when his translations have been certified.

Also from BTTS:

With One Heart Bowing to the City of Ten Thousand Buddhas, Vol. I, Paperbound, with photos, 173 pages.

Listen to Yourself, Think Everything Over, Instruction in meditation and recitation.

Pure Land and Ch'an Dharma Talks, paperbound 72 pages.

Records of the Life of the Ven. Master Hsüan Hua, Vol. I, paperbound, 96 pages.

Records of the Life of the Venerable Master Hsüan Hua, Vol. II, paperbound, 229 pages.

World Peace Gathering, paperbound, 128 pages.

Three Steps One Bow, paperbound 156 pages.

The Ten Dharma Realms are Not Beyond a Single Thought, paperbound 72 pages.

Celebrisi's Journey, paperbound, 178 pages.

A BRIGHT STAR IN A TROUBLED WORLD:

THE CITY OF TEN THOUSAND BUDDHAS

Located at Talmage, California, just south of
Ukiah and about two hours north of San Francisco, is
Wonderful Enlightenment Mountain. Situated at the base
is the 237 acre area holding 60 buildings which is
called the City of Ten Thousand Buddhas which is fast
becoming a center for religious, educational, and
social programs for world Buddhism.

At present, the complex houses Tathagata Monastery
and the Great Compassion House for men, Great Joyous
Giving House for women, the campus of Dharma Realm
Buddhist University, and a large auditorium. Plans are
underway to present many kinds of programs to benefit
people in spirit, mind, and body--a home for the aged,
a hospital emphasizing the utilization of both eastern
and western healing techniques, an alternative mental
health facility, and educational programs ranging from
pre-school through Ph.D. Cottage industries, organic
farming, and living in harmony with our environment
will be stressed. The City is an ideal spot for
conventions where people of all races and religions
can exchange their ideas and unite their energies to

A Dharma lecture in the Hall of Ten Thousand Buddhas

promote human welfare and world peace.

Religious cultivation will be foremost and the City will be instrumental in the transmission of the orthodox precepts of the Buddhas, thus developing Bhikshus and Bhikshunis to teach and maintain the Buddhadharma. Rigorous cultivation sessions are held regularly and the grounds of the monastery provide a pure and quiet setting to pursue the study of meditation. A number of facilities are available for those found qualified to retreat into contemplative seclusion. The spacious grounds have more than a hundred acres of pine groves, and a running stream.

At a time when the world is torn with strife, the City of Ten Thousand Buddhas appears as a guiding star for all of us to discover life's true meaning and pass it on to future generations.

The four-fold assembly of disciples: City of Ten Thousand Buddhas

DHARMA REALM BUDDHIST UNIVERSITY

A SPECIAL APPROACH

Focus on Values: examining the moral foundations of ancient spiritual traditions, relating those traditions to space-age living, and finding what it takes to live in harmony with our social and natural environments.

Focus on change: a key to understanding ourselves, our relationships, and the crises of the modern world. What we seek is to be open to new ways of seeing ourselves, to new modes of relating to friend and stranger, and to new methods and technological aids that supplement and open up for us the limitless store of human wisdom, past and present.

Total environment education where teacher and student are partners in the educational process and share responsibility for it. Learning takes place both in and out of the classroom in a community which is concerned with the complex problems of society.

Personally tailored programs in which education need not be constricted by traditional department boundries. The emphasis will be on meaningful learning, not just the accumulation of facts and test-taking skills.

Education for young and old where the different generations come together to share in the experience of learning and thereby enrich that experience. The University also especially encourages those with valuable life experience to apply for special experimental learning credits.

GUIDING IDEALS

These are the ideals which will guide education at Dharma Realm University:

To explain and share the Buddha's teaching;
To develop straightforward minds and hearts;
To benefit society;
To encourage all beings to seek enlightenment.

524

CAMPUS

The main campus of Dharma Realm University is located at the foot of Cow Mountain National Recreation Area in the Beautiful Ukiah valley. It is surrounded by the woods, meadows, and farmland of the City of Ten Thousand Buddhas.

The University will be housed in several large buildings set among trees and broad lawns. One classroom building has been newly refurbished for educational use.

The air is clean and fresh, and the climate is pleasant and temperate (av. min. temp. 43.2 deg: av. max. temp. 76 deg.) Rarely falling below freezing in the winter and usually dry in the summer, the area is very fertile with much grape and fruit tree cultivation. Close by are the Russian River, Lake Mendocino and Clear Lake, several hot springs, redwood and other national forest lands, and the scenic Pacific Coast.

PROGRAMS-*Undergraduate and graduate, full-time and part-time*

The University intends to provide quality education in a number of fields, with   emphasis (wherever possible) on matching classroom theory with practical experience. The curriculum is divided into three main areas:

The Letters and Science Program: In addition to a regular curriculum of Humanities, Social, and Natural Sciences, special emphasis will be laid on East-West studies, with strong offerings in Asian languages, literature, philosophy, and religion. We expect pioneering interdisciplinary approaches in many of these areas, combining the best of Asian and Western approaches to education. Education for personal growth and the development of special competencies will be the twin aims of the program.

The Buddhist Studies Program will emphasize a combination of traditional and modern methods including actual practice of the Buddhadharma as well as scholarly investigation. Offerings will range from introductory fundamentals to advanced meditation and will include advanced seminars in both English and canonical languages.

The Arts Program: Practical Arts will concentrate on putting knowledge to work right away in workshops for building a living community ecology, energy, gardening and nutrition, community planning, management, etc. Creative Arts offerings will include the meeting of East and West in a whole panorama of studio arts. There will be special courses in Chinese calligraphy, in the creation of Buddha images, and in music. Individual Arts workshops will include t'ai-chi ch'uan, yoga, meditational techniques, wilderness survival, and much more.

THE INTERNATIONAL TRANSLATION CENTER

The Translation Center will sponsor courses, workshops, and special programs concerned with translation techniques for a wide range of languages and will coordinate a unique degree program in translation.

THE WORLD RELIGIONS CENTER

The World Religions Center will sponsor workshops, conferences, and other special programs to aid in mutual understanding and good will among those of different faiths.

SPECIAL INTERNATIONAL STUDENT PROGRAM

In the future, there will be special emphasis on welcoming students from Asian countries to complement the University's strong offerings in East-West studies. Areas of special interest to Asian students will be added to the curriculum as well as a strong English as a Second Language (ESL) Program.

DONATIONS

Dharma Realm University welcomes your help with donations. In addition to financial assistance, the University needs home and office furniture, books and scholarly journals, supplies and equipment, and the services of volunteers. *All donations are tax deductable.*

VERSE ON RETURNING THE LIGHT

Truly recognize your own faults
And don't discuss the faults of others.
Other's faults are just your own faults,
Being one with everyone
is called great compassion.

— Ven. Master Hsuan Hua

OUTLINE FOR CHAPTER TWO:
EXPEDIENT DEVICES

OUTLINE FOR CHAPTER TWO: EXPEDIENT DEVICES

by Dharma Master Ngou-i

Sequential numbers shown at left below correspond to numbers shown throughout the sutra text to indicate outline headings.

```
1.   C2  The branches division of the sutra.
2.  .D1  General explanation: opening the three and revealing the one.
3.  ..E1  Generally opening and revealing.
4.  ...F1  Lauding the Buddhas' Two Wisdoms.
5.  ....G1  Prose.
6.  .....H1  Praising the Two Wisdoms with words.
7.  ......I1  Describing the provisional and actual wisdom of all Buddhas.
8.  .......J1  Acclaiming both types of wisdom.
9.  .......J2  Describing the foundation of both types of wisdom.
10. .......J3  Conclusion.
11. ......I2  Describing the provisional and actual wisdom of Shakyamuni
                Buddha.
12. .......J1  Acclaiming both types of wisdom.
13. .......J2  Describing the foundation of both types of wisdom.
14. .......J3  Conclusion.
15. .....H2  Praising the Two Wisdoms as being beyond description.
16. ......I1  Basis for this praise.
17. .......J1  Basis.
18. .......J2  That which is beyond description.
19. ......I2  The actual praise of stopping the explanation.
20. .......J1  Stopping.
21. .......J2  The reason for stopping.
22. ....G2  Verse.
23. .....H1  Praising the Two Wisdoms.
24. ......I1  Praising both types of wisdom of all Buddhas and Shakyamuni
                Buddha.
```

532